EASTERN REGION—Continued
PHILADELPHIA TERMINAL DIVISION—Continued

			Dist. from Jer. City (Pass. Sta.)
		Frankford, Pa. (Frankford Coal & Supply Co., Inc.)†	79.3
		" (Yale & Towne Mfg. Co.)†	79.3
		" (Smedley & Bro.)†	79.3
		" (Station)‡	79.4
80		" (Geo. B. Newton Coal Co. No. 1, and Red Star Fuel Co.)†	79.6
		" (Wm. & Harvey Rowland Inc., No. 1, and Geo. W. Meckert)†	79.6
		" ("Ford" Tower)	79.9
		" (Robert H. Foerderer Nos. 1 & 2)†	79.9
		Frankford Jc., Pa. (Junc. P. & T. R. R., and Conn. Ry.)*	79.9
		" (Storage)‖	79.9
		" (Hulton Dyeing Co. No. 2)†	80.2
		" (Hulton Dyeing Co. No. 1)†	80.2
		" (Station)*‡	80.4
		" (Phila. Wool Scouring & Carbonizing Co.)†	80.6
81		" ("Shore" Tower)	80.6
		" (Maurice J. Crean)†	80.7
		" (Boger & Crawford)†	81.0
		" (Junc. D. R. R. R. & B. Co.)*‡	80.6
		" (Frankford Junction Engine Terminal)‖	81.0
		" (Junc. Kensington Br.—E. Conn.)*‡	81.2
		" (Penna.-New Jersey State Line)	82.6
1183		"Jersey" Tower (Jc. Atlantic Div.)*	83.2
		Frankford Jc., Phila., Pa. (P. & T. R. R. and C. Ry.)*	80.0
81		" (Scales)	80.2
		Ontario St., Phila., Pa. (American Engineering Co. Nos. 5 & 6)†	80.2
		" (American Engineering Co. No. 4)†	80.2
		" (Allegheny Iron & Metal Co.)†	80.4
0402A		" (Wm. & Harvey Rowland, Inc. No. 2)†	80.5
		" (Wm. & Harvey Rowland, Inc. No. 3)†	80.5
		" (Frankford Junction Engine Terminal)‖	80.3
		Ontario St., Phila., Pa. (Schlicter Jute Cordage Co.)†	80.3
		" (Jc. D. R. R. R. & B. Co.)‖	80.4
		" (Jc. Frankford Street Branch)	80.4
		" (Butler St. Siding)‖	80.5
		" (Belmont Packing & Rubber Co.)†	80.6
		" (Army Air Forces Specialized Depot)†	80.6
0403		" (J & L Steel Barrel Co.)†	80.6
		" (Erie Avenue Siding)‖	80.9
		" (Hulburt Oil & Grease Co.)†	80.9
		" (F. W. Tunnell & Co. No. 4)†	80.9
		" (F. W. Tunnell & Co. Nos. 1, 2 & 3)†	80.9
		" (F. W. Tunnell & Co. No. 5)†	81.1
		" (Independent Mfg. Co.)†	81.1
		" (Wheatsheaf Lane Passing)‖	81.2
		" (Roxborough Street)	81.4

* No Siding
† For individual use
‖ Siding—No carload delivery
‡ Telephone Office
‡ Telegraph Office

EASTERN REGION—Continued
PHILADELPHIA TERMINAL DIVISION—Continued

(Frankford St. Br.—Connecting Ry.—Cont.)

		Dist. from Jer. City (Pass. Sta.)
	Ontario St., Phila., Pa. (Jos. Berliner Co.)†	81.5
	" (Bers & Co., and Penna. Foundry Supply & Sand Co.)†	81.5
0404	" (Morris, Wheeler & Co. No. 1—Montgomery Div.)†	81.7
	" (Martin Coal & Coke Co.)†	81.6
	" (Pearce St. Public Dely., Murray Oil Products Co., Merchants Chemical Co., John N. Williams & Co., and Quaker City Hide Co.†)	81.9
	Ontario St., Phila., Pa. (Barrett Co. Nos. 1 & 2)†	82.0
0405	" (Barrett Co. No. 3)†	82.1
	" (Barrett Co. No. 4)†	82.1
	" (Barrett Co. No. 5)†	82.1
0402	Kensington, Phila., Pa. (Jc. K. & T. Branch)*	81.1

(PHILADELPHIA & TRENTON RAILROAD—Continued — Westmoreland Street Branch)

		Dist. from Jer. City (Pass. Sta.)
	Ontario St., Phila., Pa. (Junc. Westmoreland St. Branch)*	80.9
	" (George Senn)†	81.0
	" (Food Fair Stores, Inc.)†	81.1
	" (David Lupton's Sons Co.)†	81.1
	" (Ontario Street Yard and Freight Station)	81.3
	" (Michael Flynn Mfg. Co., and Michael Flynn, Inc.)†	81.1
	" (Service Syndicate, Inc.)†	81.3
0414	" (Haskell-Dawes Machine Co., Inc., and Friel & Bernheim Co.)†	81.3
	" (Geo. Sall Metals Co.)†	81.2
	" (M. J. Hunt, Sons)†	81.2
	" (Edgar T. Ward Sons Co.)†	81.3
	" (Daniel Buck, Inc.)†	81.3
	" (General Smelting Co.)†	81.9
	" (Ontario Land Co.)†ᵏ	81.9
	" (Enterprise Oil Co., Enterprise Animal Oil Co., and Enterprise Tallow & Grease Co.)†ᵏ	81.9
	" (Mutual Rendering Co., Inc.)†ᵏ	81.9
	Ontario St., Phila., Pa. (Gill Glass & Fixture Co.)†	80.7
	" (Klein Stove Co., and Caloric Gas Stove Works)†	80.9
0415	" (Owen Letter's Sons Nos. 1 & 2)†	80.9
	" (Scholler Bros., Inc.)†	81.1
	" (Masland Duraleather Co.)†	81.1
	" (Allegheny Ave.)*	81.1
	" (Allegheny Dye Works—Brehm & Stehle)†	81.2
0416	Junc. Delaware Ave. Branch*	81.9
	Ontario St., Phila., Pa. (Geo. B. Newton Coal Co. No. 2)†	82.0
0415A	" (Kensington Hygeia Ice Co., Geo. B. Newton Coal Co. No. 3, and Baseman Coal & Coke Co.)†	82.1

* No Siding
† For individual use
ᵏ Connection with P. B. L. R. R.

EASTERN REGION—Continued
PHILADELPHIA TERMINAL DIVISION—Continued

(CONNECTING RAILWAY—Continued — Oxford Road Branch)

		Dist. from Jer. City (Pass. Sta.)
82	Junction Oxford Road Branch*	81.9
	North Penn, Phila., Pa. (Storage)‖	82.2
	" (Globe Union, Inc.)†	82.2
	" (Grinnell Co., Inc.)†	82.3
	" (Selas Co.)†	82.3
	" (Maneely Warehouse—E. G. Budd Mfg. Co. No. 10)†	82.4
	" (Atlantic Elevator Co.)†	82.4
	" (Wickwire-Spencer Steel Co. and Phila. Iron Works, Inc.)†	82.4
	" (H. J. Heinz Co.)†	82.4
	" (Messinger Bearings, Inc. and Geo. Livingston)†	82.4
	" (Warren-Ehret Co.)†	82.5
	" (Jos. H. Collins & Son)†	82.5
	" (Crescent Box Corp.)†	82.5
	" (F. C. Castelli Co.)†	82.5
1141	" (Gibson-Walker Co. No. 1)†	82.5
	" (Gibson-Walker Co. No. 2)†	82.6
	" (General Utilities Corp.)†	82.8
	" (Mack Paving & Construction Co.)†	82.4
	" (Phila. Electric Co. No. 7)†	82.5
	" (Barber Asphalt Co. No. 1)†	82.6
	" (Keebler-Weyl Baking Co. No. 1)†	82.6
	" (Keebler-Weyl Baking Co. No. 2)†	82.7
	" (Storage)‖	82.6
	" (Jacob R. Fox, Jr., Flemming & Bates Coal Co. No. 2, and Jafolla & Massa Cut Stone Co.)†	82.6
	" (Barber Asphalt Co. No. 2)†	82.6
	" (Walter E. Knipe & Sons)†	83.4
	" (Friends Hospital, Phila., Pa.)†	83.8
	Sears, Phila., Pa. (Freight Station)‖	84.4
	" (Sears Roebuck & Co. No. 3)†	84.2
	" (Junc. Reading Co.)‖	84.6
1144	" (Benjamin Franklin Paint & Varnish Co.)†	85.1
	" (Sears Roebuck & Co. No. 4—Power Plant)†	85.1
	" (Strick Co.)†	84.6
	" (U.S. Naval Aviation Supply Depot)†	84.6
	" (John Hagan Co. Inc.)†	85.0
	Oxford Road, Pa. (Public Delivery)	85.3
1145	" (Simpson & Brown)†	85.3
	" (Ralph W. Gebron)†	85.3
	North Penn, Phila., Pa. (Fairhill Yard—West End—Storage)‖	81.9
83	" (SKF Industries, Inc. No. 1)†	81.9
	" (Sloane-Blabon Corp.)†	81.9
	" (Junc. Fairhill Branch)	81.9

(Via Reading Co. Frankford Br.)

* No Siding
† For individual use
‖ Siding—No carload delivery

PENNSYLVANIA RAILROAD
FACILITIES In Color

Volume 3: PHILADELPHIA DIVISION

by Robert J. Yanosey

Copyright © 2009
Morning Sun Books, Inc.

All rights reserved. This book may not be reproduced in part or in whole without written permission from the publisher, except in the case of brief quotations or reproductions of the cover for the purposes of review.

To access our full library *In Color* visit us at
www.morningsunbooks.com

Morning Sun Books Inc.

ROBERT J. YANOSEY, President

Published by
Morning Sun Books, Inc.
9 Pheasant Lane
Scotch Plains, NJ 07076
Printed in Korea

Library of Congress
Catalog Card No. 2008921805

First Printing
ISBN 1-58248-255-1

Above and Page 1 - *Passenger traffic has but the outside mains to skirt some Philadelphia Division freight congestion in May 1970. The location? A mile east of North Philadelphia station, at milepost 83.9 to be precise, as determined by the "C.H. Wheeler Mfg. Co." entry in the road's C.T.1000. Auxiliary sidings and spurs were a major component of any railroad's facilities. Created in a time when individual freight cars were spotted at a customer's loading dock, their combined mileage and switches rivaled that of the main routes. The PRR had a system to list these stations and sidings, its C.T. 1000 booklet. A Division-appropriate selection of Philadelphia Division pages from the final 1945 edition is shown on the end sheets.*

(William Rosenberg)

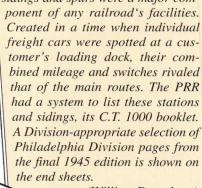

DEDICATION

*Our third volume
is dedicated to*

RICH FAGIN

*Train Collector,
PRR Fan and Friend.*

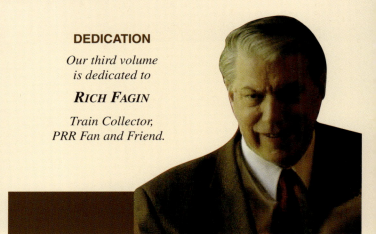

ACKNOWLEDGEMENTS

When one sits down to examine the several hundred color images in this volume, it should be understood that each is just a fraction of a second of 177 years of Pennsylvania Railroad history. With much practice and a skilled eye, our photographer composed his chosen scene; an image that we are so grateful to reproduce within this book. But consider what else lay trackside that day: PRR Standard signage, signals, telephone boxes, bridges, trestles, culverts, and a host of buildings that might range from signal tower, to passenger station, to yard and shop buildings. There was much to record! So for focusing on our subject, let us extend our sincere appreciation to these photographers: William J. Brennan, Will Coxey, John Dziobko, Jr., Steve Eisenman, Robert Fillman, Matt Herson, Al Holtz, the Kantner Brothers - Arch and Bruce, Gerald H. Landau, George M. Leilich, Dr. Art Peterson, Allan H. Roberts, William M. Rosenberg, James P. Shuman, Harold A. Smith, John P. Stroup, Rich Taylor, Bill Tilden, Frank Watson and Walter Zullig. In addition George Conrad, Will Coxey, Mitch Dakelman and Ralph Phillips graciously lent assistance in one form or another.

This volume continues the *PRR Facilities* series into the Philadelphia Division, an area extraordinarily rich in PRR history The diverse facilities serving both through and commuter passenger operations, main line and local freight, and heavy industrial and port areas provides a multifaceted tapestry of subject material.

There is more to railroading than trains!

Robert J. Yanosey
August 1, 2008

FOREWORD

PENNSYLVANIA RAILROAD FACILITIES In Color
Volume 3: PHILADELPHIA DIVISION

HISTORICAL BACKGROUND

In its early years the Pennsylvania Railroad was a Philadelphia corporation in every way but one. Although it opened offices there shortly after its founding in 1846, it didn't actually own trackage into the city until 11 years later when it purchased the Philadelphia & Columbia RR in 1857, and the canal portions of the Main Line of Public Works from the Commonwealth of Pennsylvania. This line gave PRR direct access to the City of Brotherly Love from the west, and making the connection with its original right-of-way running westward from Harrisburg. It then went on to establish the critical connection from Philadelphia northward to New York City by leasing the United New Jersey Railroads in 1871, and from Philadelphia south to Baltimore (and later Washington, D.C.) 10 years later by triumphantly winning the fierce political and financial battle for ownership of the Philadelphia, Wilmington & Baltimore Railroad from its arch-rival, the Baltimore & Ohio.

* * *

Turning to the northern connection into Philadelphia, PRR took over the Philadelphia & Trenton as part of the lease of the United New Jersey Railroad and Canal Company in 1871, but it is important to understand the events preceding that lease to grasp the significance of this particular route. The original Philadelphia & Trenton depot serving Philadelphia was located in the Kensington area northeast of the main business district. This location required passengers and freight to be transported across the city to PRR's depot in West Philadelphia, resulting in considerable expense and delay.

To resolve this problem, and to establish a direct north-south connection through the city, PRR entered into negotiations in 1862 with the Joint Companies (P&T, Camden & Amboy, New Jersey Rail Road and Transportation Co. and the Delaware & Raritan Canal Co.) for operating rights on the P&T and C&A extension. The P&T would then gain access to PRR's West Philadelphia station by means of a new line to be built by PRR. This 6.5-mile line, completed in 1867, ran from Mantua, just north of PRR's new station in West Philadelphia, to Frankford Junction with the P&T. The Connecting Railway, as it was named, firmly established not only the primary rail route between Philadelphia and New York on the west side of the Delaware, but also the location of future PRR stations serving the city.

Traffic over this line was heavy almost from the start. The Connecting Railway was initially double track; however, with the rapidly growing traffic it was four-tracked from Germantown Junction (later North Philadelphia) to the Schuylkill River Bridge in 1882, and subsequently eastward to Frankford Junction as an elevated right-of-way completed in 1889. A fifth (No. 5) and sixth (0 Track) were subsequently added.

* * *

A second critical piece of trackage in establishing not only a direct north-south route through the city but also a southern connection was the Junction Railroad. Prior to completion of this line, goods and passengers (including military personnel during the Civil War) were moved between stations though the congested city streets. The Pennsylvania Legislature chartered the Junction Railroad Company, a joint venture of PRR, the Philadelphia, Wilmington and Baltimore and the Reading. The three-mile line was built along the west bank of the Schuylkill River in stages, finally completed in 1866. This line in turn precipitated five years of conflict and intrigue between PRR and the B&O-Reading for control of the PW&B, finally resulting in PRR's successful takeover of the line in 1881.

It had taken 25 years to achieve success, but PRR had become the premiere railroad serving Philadelphia, with major lines extending northward to New York City, westward to Pittsburgh and beyond, and southward, ultimately to the nation's capital.

With Center City, Philadelphia beckoning ahead, eastbound Metroliner #120 sweeps past Arsenal Tower on July 22, 1972. (William M. Tilden)

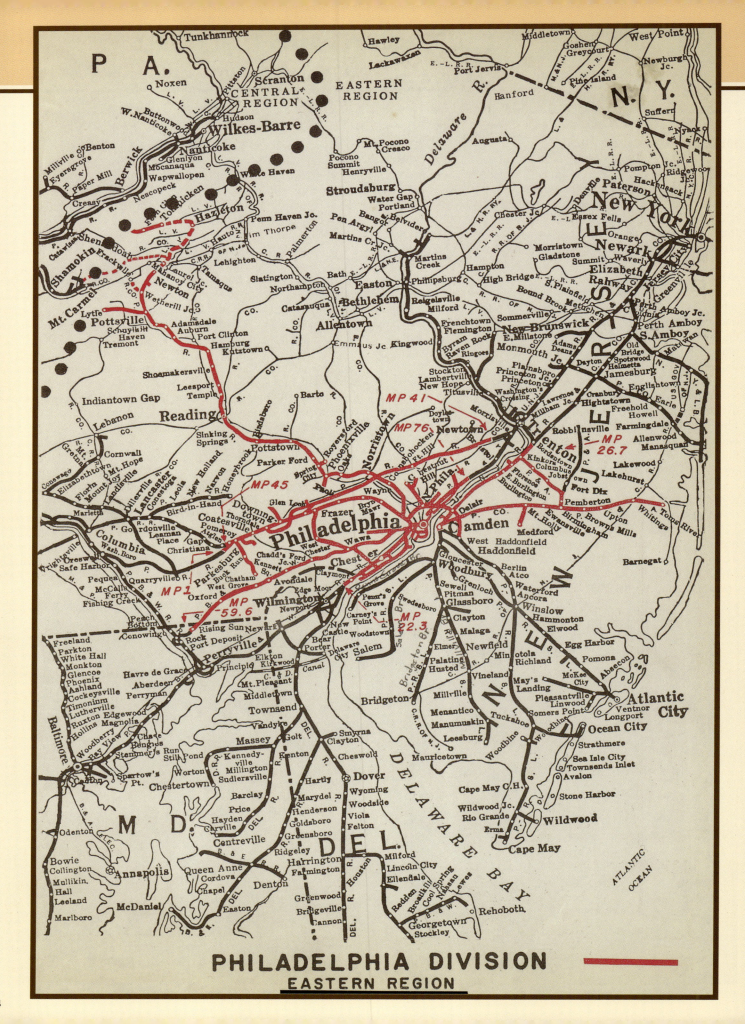

PENNSYLVANIA RAILROAD FACILITIES In Color

Volume 3: PHILADELPHIA DIVISION

TABLE OF CONTENTS

FOREWORD 3

MAIN LINE
HOLMESBURG JUNCTION TO ZOO TOWER 6
- Holmesburg Junction 6
- Holmes Tower 6
- Wissinoming 7
- Bridesburg 7
- Frankford 7
- Frankford Junction 8
- Shore Tower 9
- North Philadelphia 10
- (Bridge 84.51) 10
- Bridge 84.69 10
- North Philadelphia Tower 12
- Bridge 86.98 14
- Bridge 87.1 14
- Zoo Tower 15

MAIN LINE
ZOO TOWER TO CENTER CITY PHILADELPHIA 18
- West Philadelphia 18
- Penn Coach Yard 19
- Race Street Engine Terminal . . . 19
- Broad Street Station 20
- Suburban Station 23
- 30th Street Station 26
- Bridge 0.76 29
- MU Storage Yard 30
- General Post Office 31

MAINE LINE
PHILADELPHIA TO BELLEVUE, DELAWARE 32
- Arsenal Tower 33
- Brill Tower 33
- Darby 34
- Curtis Park 34
- Folcroft 34
- Glenolden 35
- Crum Lynne 35
- Baldwin Tower 35
- Eddystone 36
- Chester 36
- Hook Tower 37
- Standard Passenger Shelter 38
- Standard Concrete Watch Box . . 38
- Standard Whistle Sign 38

CHESTNUT HILL BRANCH 39
- North Philadelphia 39
- Chelten Avenue 40
- Tulpehocken 40
- Allen Lane 41
- St. Martins 41
- Austin Tower 42
- Chestnut Hill 42

WEST CHESTER BRANCH 44
- Fernwood-Yeadon 44
- Lansdowne 45
- Clifton-Aldan 47
- Morton-Rutledge 47
- Swarthmore 48
- Wallingford 49
- Media 50
- Wawa 51
- Glen Mills 51
- Cheyney 52
- West Chester 53

WEST PHILADELPHIA ELEVATED BRANCH / DELAWARE EXTENSION 54
- High Line 54
- Arsenal Bridge 55
- Stadium Tower 56
- Greenwich Point Yard 57
- Girard Point Elevator 58
- Coal Pier 59
- Warming Shed 60
- Ore Pier 60
- Conveyor System 61
- Distribution Tower 61
- Transfer Facility 62
- Delaware Avenue 63
- Delaware Avenue Branch 64
- Market Street Ferry Terminal . . 65
- Federal Street Terminal 66

BORDENTOWN BRANCH / BORDENTOWN SECONDARY . . 67
- Burlington 67
- Bridge 12.3 68
- Riverside 69
- Palmyra 69
- Delair 69
- Pavonia Yard 70
- Pavonia Yard Enginehouse 71
- Center Tower 71
- Camden 72
- Camden Terminal Enginehouse . 72

DELAWARE RIVER RAILROAD & BRIDGE COMPANY 74
- Delair Bridge 74
- Jersey Tower 75
- Jordan 75

PEMBERTON BRANCH / BIRMINGHAM SECONDARY . . 76
- Broadway Station 76
- Pavonia Yard 77
- Bridge 6.62 77
- Moorestown 78
- Bridge 13.59 79
- Mount Holly 80
- Birmingham 81
- Pemberton 81
- Toms River 82

MAIN LINE
ZOO TOWER TO PARKESBURG 83
- New York-Pittsburgh Subway . . 84
- Bridge 3.03 84
- 52nd Street Yards 84
- 46th Street Engine Terminal . . . 85
- Overbrook Tower 86
- Overbrook 86
- Merion 87
- Narberth 87
- Wynnewood 88
- Ardmore 89
- Haverford 90
- Bryn Mawr 91
- Bryn Mawr Tower 92
- Rosemont 93
- Villanova 93
- St. Davids 96
- Wayne 96
- Strafford 97
- Devon 98
- Berwyn 98
- Daylesford 98
- Paoli 100
- Paoli Tower 103
- Paoli Car Shop 106
- Bridge 28.85 107
- Thorn Tower 108
- Coatesville 110
- Park Tower 110
- Parkesburg 111
- telegraph pole 111

TRENTON BRANCH 112
- Bridge 21.91 112
- Plymouth Meeting 112

SCHUYLKILL BRANCH 113
- Wynnefield Avenue 113
- Bala 114
- Cynwyd 114
- Barmouth 115
- Bridge 7.70 116
- Manayunk 117
- PRR Substation 118
- Shawmont 118
- Miquon 118
- Spring Mill 119
- Conshohocken 120
- Earnest 120
- Norris Tower 120
- Norristown 121
- Haws Avenue 122
- Phoenixville 122
- Pottstown 122
- Birdsboro 123
- Brooke Tower 123
- Birdsboro Freight House . . . 124
- Reading 125
- Bridge 58.30 125
- Reading Tower 125
- Reading Freight House 125
- Shoemakersville 126
- Mt. Carbon Enginehouse . . . 126
- Carbon 127
- Darkwater Trestle 128

This PRR map issued March 1, 1964 shows the Philadelphia Division as of that date. This third volume in the continuing *PRR Facilities* series covers the north-south main line from the division post with the New York Division at MP 76.0 (from Jersey City) into 30th Street and Suburban Stations in Philadelphia (with a fond look back at Broad Street Station). It continues southward to the division post with the Chesapeake Division at MP 22.2 (from Suburban Station), just south of Bellevue, Delaware. The Philadelphia area was laced with branches radiating out from the city: this volume looks at three suburban commuter lines in Pennsylvania – the Chestnut Hill, West Chester and Schuylkill Branches, plus the freight-only trackage on the Trenton Cutoff and the High Line continuing onto the Delaware Extension to the port facilities. Also covered are two lines in New Jersey, the Bordentown and Pemberton Branches, the latter extending to Toms River on the Birmingham Secondary Track. We then move westward from the junction with the north-south main at Zoo Tower and examine the facilities on the east-west main (including *the* legendary Main Line) westward to Parkesburg and finally the Schuylkill Branch.

Historic Philadelphia was the nation's third largest city in April 1948 when PRR produced this 12-panel brochure promoting tourism. In addition to Rittenhouse Square, the Philadelphia Museum of Art, and Independence Hall, the pamphlet mapped out the street locations of several PRR stations. Twenty years later, Broad Street Station, Market Street Wharf, Camden Terminal and indeed PRR itself were but fading memories.
(Morning Sun Books Collection)

MAIN LINE

HOLMESBURG JUNCTION TO ZOO TOWER

The PRR mainline in this first section is composed of two segments – the first follows essentially the north-south route of the Philadelphia and Trenton Railroad, although some realignment occurred when the line was elevated in 1891-95 to eliminate many grade crossings. The second section is the east-west line of the PRR Connecting Railway from Frankford Junction west to Zoo Tower across the Schuylkill River.

Interlocking	Interlocking Station	Block Station	MAIN LINE	Distance from Jersey City
			DIVISION POST (N. Y. Division)	76
X	X	X-O	HOLMESBURG JCT.	77
			HOLMES	77
			TACONY	78
			WISSINOMING	79
			BRIDESBURG	80
X	X	X-O	FRANKFORD	80
			FORD	81
			FRANKFORD JCT.	81
X	X	X-O	SHORE	82
			NORTH PHILADELPHIA	85
X	X	X-O	NORTH PHILADELPHIA	85
X	X	X-O	ZOO	88
			*Distance from Suburban Station.	*
X	X	X-O	ZOO (44th St.)	3
			52nd STREET	3
X			VALLEY—R-Overbrook	4
X	X	X-O	OVERBROOK	5
			OVERBROOK	5
			MERION	6
			NARBERTH	6
			WYNNEWOOD	7
			ARDMORE	8
			HAVERFORD	9
			BRYN MAWR	10
X	B	B	BRYN MAWR	10
			ROSEMONT	10
			VILLANOVA	12
			RADNOR	13
			ST. DAVIDS	13
			WAYNE	14
			STRAFFORD	15
			DEVON	16
			BERWYN	17
			DAYLESFORD	18
			PAOLI	19
X	X	X	PAOLI	19
			MALVERN	21
			FRAZER	23
X			GLEN—R-Thorn	25
			WHITFORD	28
X			DOWNS—R-Thorn	32
			DOWNINGTOWN	32
X	X	X	THORN	35
			THORNDALE	35
X			CALN—R-Thorn	36
			COATESVILLE	38
			POMEROY	41
X	X	X-O	PARK	43
			PARKESBURG	44
			DIVISION POST (Harrisburg Division)	45

Holmesburg, the first community on the line south of the New York Division Post, was named after Thomas Holme, surveyor and friend of William Penn, who drew the first map of Philadelphia. Holmesburg had been a part of Delaware Township, Philadelphia County, prior to the Act of Consolidation incorporating it within the city limits in 1854. It was the birthplace of Matthias Baldwin, founder of Philadelphia's famed Baldwin Locomotive Works.

The passenger stations built along the PRR mainline north of Philadelphia in the late 19th Century reflected the well-heeled clientele that lived in the upscale residential areas in the northeast section of the city at that time. The station named **Holmesburg Junction** (MP 77.2 from Jersey City on the New York Division) was a two-story structure built in 1886 on the west side of the tracks. Holmes Tower was located on the east side. The current brick structure located on the west side is a combination of a two-story portion that houses the tower and an attached single-story ticket office and southbound waiting room, with a brick shelter on the northbound side. The station and tower are shown here in November 1969, with a 12-car string of Penn Central Silverliners headed southward to the Army-Navy Game in South Philadelphia.
(Will Coxey, West Jersey Chapter NRHS Collection)

A closer view of **Holmes Tower** as it appeared on July 12, 1970. Note that the station sign is a classic PRR keystone design painted over by Penn Central. The tower housed an electro-mechanical machine to control the universal set of crossovers on the four-track main and the junction with the freight-only Bustleton Branch (hence the name "Junction") serving several industries to the northwest. (John P. Stroup)

The original two-story station (a Type 2B-2) at **Wissinoming** (MP 79.3 – not to be confused with Wyomissing on the Schuylkill Branch) was built in 1889 and was subsequently replaced with these two brick shelters. Our photographer stepped out onto the right-of-way to catch a northbound pair, of Silverliner II's, with their as-delivered keystone logos in August 1967 – and recorded his shadow for posterity as well. *(William Rosenberg)*

It's now September 1978 – the station is unchanged except Penn Central has repainted the keystone station sign. The new GE-built Silverliner IV's (delivered in 1974-5) have both the original SEPTA and Penn Central logos. *(Harold A. Smith)*

Bridesburg (MP 80.1) was incorporated as a borough on April 1, 1848. It was initially called Kirkbridesburg after Joseph Kirkbride, who operated an early ferry service across the Delaware River to New Jersey and later built a bridge over Frankford Creek. Like other communities in the area north of the city, the borough was annexed by the City of Philadelphia in the 1854 consolidation. The name was changed to its current form after the Civil War by the local citizens who felt that the original name was too long.

A Conrail Frankford Junction Yard-based drill rolls past the brick shelters in October 1979 – these shelters replaced a two-story station constructed in 1896 near the location of an early freight depot built by the P&T in 1845. Through freight operations on this section of the line were drastically curtailed after the completion of the Trenton Cutoff (later Trenton Branch) freight bypass in 1892.
(Harold A. Smith)

Another basic brick shelter served as the southbound station at **Frankford** (MP 80.9), shown in a November 1969 view. Again, it replaced a substantial two-story structure with a platform canopy built in 1883 on the northbound side and a matching shelter on the southbound side in 1886. Frankford was founded in 1684 by German settlers and was named after the Frankfort Company, which built a plant there along what was then known as Tacony Creek, later Frankford. William Penn laid out a road through the village that ran from the original center of Philadelphia to his homestead Pennsbury Manor in Bucks County and on to New York City. This road became known as the Frankford Pike, later Frankford Avenue, and the main thoroughfare of the community. The village was incorporated as a borough in 1800 and annexed by the City of Philadelphia in 1854.

There were multiple road crossings at grade within this area when the P&T was constructed. Over time a few were eliminated, but a major grade crossing elimination program was begun by PRR in 1891 and essentially completed by 1895. In several sections the old right-of-way was retained as industrial trackage, while the new main tracks were elevated on a fill with plate girder bridges over the cross streets. *(William Rosenberg)*

Frankford Junction (MP 81.8) is the point where the Connecting Railway met the P&T. It initially consisted of a wye and a small freight yard along the P&T right-of-way, and the early passenger station located at the western end of the wye. This April 1961 view looks east toward the junction – a GG1 rolls a southbound train around the tight superelevated curved mainline towards Philadelphia while a pair of EMD units moves a westbound freight off the Delaware River Railroad & Bridge Co. Branch, which extends across the Delair Bridge to provide access to Atlantic City and other southern New Jersey shore points. In between Frankford Junction Yard is just visible. This yard was originally laid out in the late 1880s as a storage yard and was gradually expanded over the years to fill the area within and to the east of the wye. It handled freight traffic for the numerous industries in the Frankford area, along the Connecting Railway, and the Kensington Branch to the south. *(Gerald H. Landau Collection)*

This view taken on September 29, 1956 looks in the opposite direction. K4s #5439 eases 10 heavyweight P70 coaches into the station where a good crowd of Atlantic City race track bound passengers await. The single-story structure was built in 1896. The main tracks are at right, and in the background is the Philadelphia Transportation Company (PTC) Market-Frankford elevated transit line. *(John Dziobko, Jr.)*

Shore Tower (MP 82.1) is located on the edge of the fill and controlled the turnouts and crossovers for trains to and from New Jersey via the Delair Bridge (Delaware River Railroad and Bridge Company Branch) as well as movements of freights in and out of the south end of Frankford Junction Yard. The two-story frame structure housed a 23-lever electro-pneumatic machine. Movements to and from the other end of the yard were controlled by Ford Tower farther east (at MP 81.2), with the interlocking a mirror image of that at Shore.

These two views taken in April 1968 depict operations at the tower. The first is Conway to Pavonia symbol freight CP6 (with a tip of the engineer's cap to the photographer) led by EF25a #6062 and companion EF36 eastbound on Track #1. The second view shows an eastbound PRSL train led by Baldwin road switcher #6010 crossing over to the bridge approach tracks. Overhead is the Market-Frankford elevated transit line in and out of the city. Plate girder Bridge 81.69 supports the main tracks over Kensington Avenue.

(Both- Gerald H. Landau Collection)

North Philadelphia (MP 85.0) was a critical part of PRR passenger operations in the city. The station was opened in 1901 to serve the patrons in the growing northern part of the city and to avoid the delays of moving east-west through trains in and out of stub-ended Broad Street Station. This August 1962 view looks west through the station showing the six through tracks (0-5) plus two additional platform tracks. The main station and waiting room is on the left, with North Philadelphia Tower beyond. The plate girder bridges in the foreground (**Bridge 84.51**) carry the tracks over Broad Street. *(Steven Eisenman)*

On July 22, 1961 a westbound train led by GG1 #4902 eases into the station past the tower. The train is on the Outward Platform Track, and in the foreground is the Naught Track. Plate girder **Bridge 84.69** carries the tracks over the Reading Company mainline. *(William Volkmer, Ralph Phillips Collection)*

North Philadelphia station replaced the previous one built in 1884 at what was previously known as Germantown Junction (with the Chestnut Hill Branch). The main structure was constructed of brick with ornamental terra cotta trim. It measured 50 x 136' overall and contained a 49 x 80' waiting room. This view shows the front façade as it appeared in July 1969. *(William Rosenberg)*

With steadily increasing volume of both commuter and through trains, in 1912 PRR embarked on a program to improve the traffic flow though the station. The tracks were raised four feet, the station was enlarged and new elevated platforms were built the following year, giving the structure the appearance as shown in this September 10, 1952 view. The station had a large version of the traditional keystone station sign facing Broad Street. Parking rates have increased at least ten-fold since this time! *(John Dziobko, Jr.)*

11

A westbound train headed by GG1 #4929 in April 1968 provides a dramatic counterpoint to **North Philadelphia Tower** (MP 85.1). The two-story concrete structure was built in 1913, replacing the previous wooden one at this location. It handled all passenger trains through the station and onto the Chestnut Hill Branch, plus local freights serving the many industries and six yards in the area. It was considered one of the most difficult towers to operate in the Philadelphia area – it took two men to handle it – not only because of the high traffic volume but also the number of opposing moves. *(William Rosenberg)*

Under Penn Central a bilious coat of green paint was slapped on the upper story of the tower. In this July 22, 1975 view Amtrak Metroliner #135 moves past the tower as Train #43, THE VALLEY FORGE, pauses at the station. *(Al Holtz)*

Photographer Will Coxey was returning from a trip to West Coast in July 1956 and came away with two memorable images from the North Philadelphia platform. His family had just alighted from THE BROADWAY LIMITED and had a half hour wait for the PRSL's SEA BREEZE, a Philadelphia to Atlantic City train that would take them home to Haddonfield.

THE BROADWAY arrived exactly on time just as THE MORNING CONGRESSIONAL, Train #131 from New York for Washington, was departing. Train #28 had arrived on the Eastward Station Track (not visible on the left) while #131 is on Track #4. Note the beautiful matched set of cars that Budd Company built during the fall of 1951 for the CONGRESSIONAL and SENATOR trains. The distinctive full length Tuscan Red letter boards were later eliminated in favor of simple red keystone decals on either side of the windows.

Shortly before the SEA BREEZE arrived, Potomac Yard to Greenville Yard symbol freight MD6 passed on Track #2, the eastward freight track, with a long train including many reefers of perishables from the South. Photographer Coxey was located on the station's Outbound Platform where the woman in the red coat is patiently awaiting arrival the arrival of the SEA BREEZE on Track #1.
(Both- Will Coxey, West Jersey Chapter NRHS Collection)

Just before crossing the Schuylkill River, the PRR main traverses a little-known (and seldom-photographed) concrete and stone arch **Bridge 86.98** over the Reading. These tracks connect with the B&O main southward along the Schuylkill River and a lightly used branch into Reading Terminal in Center City. GG1 #4916 is nicely centered on the bridge as it heads northward with Train #172, THE SENATOR, on June 22, 1968. *(William M. Tilden)*

Bridge 87.1 better known as the Schuylkill River Bridge has had a long and storied history. The original bridge erected across the river when the Connecting Railway was built in 1864-67 was a double-tracked arched masonry structure with a cast iron truss spanning the middle of the river. The stonework was beautifully detailed and finished, and the deck was lined with an ornate cast iron railing and rows of decorative iron lampposts. As tonnage increased by the mid-1880s additional tension members were added to reinforce the iron truss. To accommodate further tonnage increases, in 1897 the cast iron structure was in turn replaced with a new 235' long steel Pratt truss. In true heroic PRR fashion, the task of shoving the old one aside and moving the new one into place was accomplished in a total elapsed time of 13 minutes!

But by 1910 the double-track bridge connecting the four-track New York Division to the east with the four double-track main lines to the west and southward into Philadelphia was a bottleneck resulting in a significant number of train delays in both directions. With traffic volume steadily increasing at the rate of ten per cent annually, PRR launched a major construction project to rebuild the bridge. The design called for a massive 1230' long, 11-arch masonry structure carrying <u>five</u> tracks. Construction began in 1911 and continued during both summer and winter months, the latter requiring extraordinary measures to protect the fresh mortar from freezing. Two tracks were opened in 1913, and the remaining three the following year. Here Penn Central GG1 #4898 leads Amtrak Train #84, THE SILVER METEOR, northbound across the historic structure in March 1976.

(Gerald H. Landau, William Rosenberg Collection)

Zoo Tower (MP 88.1 from the New York Division, MP 3.2 from Suburban Station in Philadelphia) was located at what can be described without hesitation as the most critical junction on the PRR system and one of the most complex rail junctions in the U.S. It was – and remains to this day – a tribute to PRR's extraordinary engineering prowess, utilizing a "flying junction" that allows key mainlines to cross and connect without interference. It consists of a wye whose three tails point northward toward New York, westward toward Pittsburgh and southward toward Philadelphia and Washington, DC.

But the key to the success of this junction are the New York and Pittsburgh Subway tunnels that duck under the legs of the wye, facilitating safe and efficient traffic flow.

This view looks northward past the tower in January 1968. The lines directly in front of the tower are the Eastward and Westward Freight Tracks, connecting to the High Line running southward through west Philadelphia. In the cut are the Belmont (freight) Branch, which was the northern end of the former Junction Railroad connecting to the Reading, and the Inward (passenger) Track to 30th Street Station. *(William Rosenberg)*

But this junction was not always such. When the Connecting Railway was first constructed, it joined the east-west main by cutting at grade across both the passenger tracks and the multiple tracks heading to the freight yards along Mantua Avenue – hence the original designation, Mantua (later New York) Junction. After a major construction effort, PRR in 1892 opened the New York Subway, a 485' stone and brick arch tunnel that allowed southbound trains from New York to move under the western leg of the wye, around the eastern leg in a cut and then under the east-west passenger and freight tracks to reach Philadelphia. A similar tunnel allowed trains between New York and Pittsburgh to safely move through the junction. Additional refinements were subsequently added to further improve traffic flow.

The setting sun shines on a northbound pair of Silverliners moving on the Outbound Track in January 1968, with the Inward Track from New York visible in the cut just to the left. At the right are Philadelphia's historic Zoological Gardens, the nation's oldest built in the 1880s from which the interlocking received its name.

(William Rosenberg)

Zoo Tower itself is a large two-story brick structure built as part of the Philadelphia Improvements in 1931. It housed a 143-lever electro-pneumatic interlocking machine which controlled the switches, signals and locks that routed traffic from three directions (north, south and west). Zoo replaced four earlier towers and was a five-man operation, interacting with five other towers nearby: North Philadelphia, Penn, A, Broad and Arsenal, as well as the Penn Coach Yard and the 46th Street Enginehouse to the west. These two views show the north and east sides of the tower in June 1969, the first with a pair of E44's moving past the tower on the Eastward Freight Track, while the second shows the lower-level wye tracks from the other direction.

Zoo saw its share of freight traffic in addition to the multitude of commuter and through passenger trains. In the second view E44 #4432 and companion with an eastbound freight ascend the grade from the Pittsburgh Subway on the Eastward Main Track toward the Schuylkill River Bridge. In the background the massive substation fills the area within the wye south of the tower. At one time the 37th Street Yard extended along the east-west tracks on the south leg of the wye, and the Mantua Freight Yard filled the space in the curve of the west leg.

(Both- William J. Brennan, Morning Sun Books Collection)

These two views taken in June 1969 show the use of Zoo Interlocking in different directions. The first provides a look at a westbound train entering the Pittsburgh Subway, as Penn Central GG1 #4931 leads Train #23, THE MANHATTAN LIMITED descending toward the tunnel. The train will pass under the east-west main and emerge from the tunnel and ascend onto the Westward Passenger Track west of the interlocking. Meanwhile Train #33, THE JUNIATA, has traversed the eastern leg of the wye on the Inward Track and continues southward toward 30th Street Station. To the left a freight rolls on the northern end of the High Line as it begins its ascent over the West Philadelphia Yards. The Philadelphia Art Museum is visible across the river in the background. *(Both- William J. Brennan)*

MAIN LINE

ZOO TOWER TO CENTER CITY PHILADELPHIA

The area along the Schuylkill River in West Philadelphia has had a long and complex history from the standpoint of railroads. The original alignment of the Philadelphia & Columbia crossed the river at Belmont to the north, but in 1849 the road took over a failed independent railroad line that was being constructed from the Market Street Bridge through West Philadelphia to the area known today as Ardmore. With an easy gradient, this right-of-way became the new alignment of the P&C, bypassing the troublesome Belmont Plane which east of the plane was sold to the Reading. This connected via the Market Street Bridge to a newly-constructed line built by the City of Philadelphia along Market Street to allow access to freight and passenger depots in the central part of the growing city. Initially, teams of horses were used to move cars, but later locomotives were allowed.

In 1861 the Junction Railroad was organized jointly by PRR, the Reading and the PW&B to allow interchange between these roads and afford a direct north-south connection through the congested city. The northern portion of this line was completed through West Philadelphia to Market Street in 1863 and subsequently became the PRR Belmont Branch.

A third main track between West Philadelphia and Overbrook on the city line was built in 1873 and a fourth track was completed in 1875 to handle the anticipated increase in traffic to and from the Centennial Exposition in Fairmount Park.

This view in **West Philadelphia** shows an inbound pair of MP54's rattling toward 30th Street Station on a warm day in October 1958. In the background a solid string of reefers rolls on the West Philadelphia Elevated Line, commonly known as the High Line. This double-track elevated line was completed in 1904 as part of Alexander Cassatt's massive 1902 Improvements Program to improve traffic flow on the entire PRR system. The structure spans the length of the yards, providing a bypass for freights to avoid the congested passenger terminal facilities. It connects the east-west and north-south mainlines at Zoo Tower with the mainline south of the city and the Delaware Extension to the port facilities in South Philadelphia. The northern portion was constructed as a brick arch viaduct, while the southern portion consists primarily of steel deck plate girder bridge spans supported on stone piers. *(Don Ball Collection)*

From its earliest days as a railroad transportation area, West Philadelphia served as the approach to the mid-18th Century depots used by PRR in Center City, the location of four later station sites, and yard and engine service facilities. The yards have changed markedly over the years. The most significant change was in 1900-05 as part of Cassatt's Improvements Program and again in the late 1920s-early 1930s under the Philadelphia Improvements. However, they have generally consisted of two areas, namely, the storage yard primarily for commuter equipment located on the broad curve approaching the Market Street Bridge crossing, and the yard for passenger cars parallel to the river. This June 1962 photo looks at the sea of Tuscan red equipment stored in **Penn Coach Yard** with GG1's and a Baldwin switcher awaiting servicing in the Race Street engine facility. *(Gerald H. Landau)*

The P&C built a roundhouse and small shop building along the main track at the northern end of West Philadelphia. Locomotive service and car shop facilities were greatly expanded during the next 20 years after the PRR purchase so that by 1876 a second roundhouse had been constructed along with the large West Philadelphia Shops, located between 30th and 32nd Streets, and a sprawling stockyard area between 30th Street and the river. In 1880 a third roundhouse was built at 31st and Spring Garden Streets. Construction of the 46th Street Enginehouse complex west of Mantua Junction in the late 1880s and its later expansion led to the gradual decline of the West Philadelphia facilities. What remained was demolished as a result of the Philadelphia Improvements in the late 1920s and '30s, but limited engine service facilities (**Race Street Engine Terminal**) were retained, as shown here on Saturday July 24, 1954. Penn Coach Yard is at left with more open tracks available on a weekend. *(John Dziobko, Jr.)*

After utilizing a variety of depots along Market Street in Philadelphia's business district in the early years, PRR built a small frame station of its own in West Philadelphia in 1858 between 30th and 31st Streets, the first of four station sites in this immediate area. With traffic increasing steadily, PRR built a larger station at this location in 1864 and closed the earlier depot at 11th and Market in the city. With the opening of the Connecting Railway in 1867, a second station was built close by, designated the "New York Depot" and the 1864 station then served east-west trains. In 1876 PRR built an expansive new terminal at 32nd and Market Streets to serve the anticipated crowds attending the Centennial Exposition, which replaced the 1864-67 depots and served as PRR's main passenger facility in Philadelphia until it was in turn supplanted by Broad Street Station in 1881. The 32nd and Market facility was subsequently destroyed in a spectacular blaze in 1896.

After the Centennial was over, PRR management led by President George Roberts concluded that the West Philadelphia location was too distant from Center City hotels and commerce, and that the road needed to re-establish its presence in the thriving business district of its home city. The decision was made to build **Broad Street Station**; a five-story brick and granite terminal building facing Philadelphia's striking new City Hall. To reach this location PRR constructed the Filbert Street Extension, made up of a double-track, three-span Howe deck truss spanning the river, a 2042' long, 60-arch brick viaduct across the city and an iron plate girder bridge over 15th Street into the terminal. Opened in 1881, the imposing but conservative Gothic structure featured a 176-foot high clock tower resembling a cathedral on the northeast corner of Broad and Filbert Streets. The head house fronted 193' along Broad Street and extended 122' to the west along Filbert and Market Streets. Twin 85' wide arched iron trainsheds covering eight passenger tracks and four tracks into a freight station extended to the west as far as 16th Street.

Broad Street Station experienced heavy traffic almost from its opening. As impressive as the terminal was, the actual trainshed area was no larger than the Centennial Station it replaced, and the acquisition of the PW&B brought trains from that road into the terminal beginning in 1882, further taxing its capacity. Movement of trains in and out of the stub-end tracks required extensive shifting of locomotives and strings of cars. With traffic reaching a million passengers a month by 1886, efforts were begun to improve the flow. The first step was to enlarge the station itself: The freight terminal was moved westward, allowing construction of an immense new trainshed 306' wide and spanning 16 tracks. Interestingly, it was actually erected over the old ones, which were subsequently demolished. The new massive trainshed covered an area over 180,000 square feet as shown in a ca. 1909 postcard view. *(Morning Sun Books Collection)*

The truly imposing new head house was 10 stories high, constructed of granite and brick and topped by an ornate tower at the corner of Broad and Market, shown here in a dramatic ca. 1948 view, looking west on Market Street. Two stories were later added to the original building to house the growing PRR headquarters staff. *(Frank Watson)*

The "Grandest Railway Terminal in America," completed in 1893, fulfilled PRR's objective to build the largest passenger station facility in the U. S. and was in keeping with its role as the Standard Railway of the World – and not, incidentally, stealing the thunder from the Reading's new terminal three blocks to the east. A grand staircase leading to the spacious 82 x 120', marble-floored main waiting room and elegant restaurant certainly had the capability to handle the patrons in style, but traffic flow still presented a problem. To improve the entrance to the terminal throat, PRR constructed two new double-track steel bridges across the river on either side of the original 1880 structure under the 1902 Improvements Program. Bridge A, built in 1902, was a 456', three-span through truss to better handle PB&W traffic from the south. Bridge B, built in the following year, was a three-span deck truss with plate girder approaches totaling 607' to serve traffic from the north and west on the new River Line constructed from Mantua Junction; it was widened to four tracks in 1910. Once these were operational, Bridge C was built in 1911 to replace the original structure. It was a 455', three-span deck truss that served primarily to move empty trains into the West Philadelphia Yards.

But handling steam trains like this one led by K4s #3675 heading out of the station in a circa 1948 view was still a time-consuming operation. Note the platform canopies installed after the trainshed was demolished following a 1923 fire. *(Frank Watson)*

The next step in solving the traffic congestion in Broad Street Station was to build two new stations to better handle through trains – North Philadelphia in 1901 for east-west trains and West Philadelphia at 32nd and Market Streets in 1903 for north-south trains. The construction of these two stations outside of the main business district would appear to represent a tacit acknowledgement by PRR management that Broad Street Station was poorly located to efficiently handle traffic other than the commuter trains into the city.

Even with these developments, traffic problems in Broad Street Station continued and actually got worse. PRR's active involvement in promoting development of Main Line suburban communities to the west brought increased commuter traffic during the peak morning and evening rush hours, further exacerbating the congestion as well as the pall of smoke in the business district. Having expanded the terminal and its approaches, a new solution was needed.

After demonstrating the successful use of electrified equipment into Penn Station in New York City, PRR management debated the merits of AC vs. DC propulsion systems and finally settled on an 11,000-volt AC catenary system for Broad Street Station and the Main Line westward to Paoli. This represented a significant decision for the future. The use of a much higher AC voltage allowed the entire system to handle not only the commuter trains, but also heavy through trains. It also necessitated the use of overhead catenary with 44,000-volt transmission lines instead of a third rail for propulsion power. The entire 20-mile project, including installation of a new position-light signal system, was completed in September 1915 at a cost of $4.5 million. Altoona Shops converted 93 steel suburban coaches into electric-powered MU cars, the famous MP54's, to operate in Main Line commuter service, replacing all 78 regularly-scheduled steam-powered by the following month.

Although some technical difficulties were encountered with arcing due to poor conduct after the passage of steam trains under the wire as well as with winter icing, the electrification program was considered a success in significantly reducing congestion in Broad Street Station. No longer did locomotives and strings of cars have to be shifted and turned for departure, greatly reducing turnaround time and effort as well as the number of locomotives needed. Electrification was extended northward onto the Connecting Railway and the Chestnut Hill Branch in 1918, and the Fort Washington Branch in 1924, and southward to the West Chester Branch and Wilmington in 1928.

The die was cast: That year President W. W. Atterbury (he was given the moniker "General" after his distinguished service as Director General of Transportation for the American Expeditionary Forces in Europe during World War I) made the dramatic announcement that the entire main line from New York to Washington, DC would be electrified. The catenary was extended to Trenton in 1930, completing the electrification of the Philadelphia commuter district. Finally, in January 1935 after a massive commitment of manpower, material and financial resources (including government loans) during the Depression (total cost $135 million) the first electric-powered mainline train made the trip from Washington to New York behind GG1 #4800, the original GG1 affectionately known as "Old Rivets," inaugurating service that continues to this day. In this view another GG1 moves a train (most likely a New York-bound CLOCKER) out of Broad Street Station on October 6, 1946, under the watchful eye of William Penn atop the 500' tower of Philadelphia City Hall, the tallest public building in the U.S. at the time. *(David Cope)*

Electrification of commuter service went a long way to solving the operational problems in Broad Street Station, but traffic continued to increase. The station served an unbelievable 500 or 1000 trains daily by the 1920s. In addition, traffic congestion in city streets made it increasingly difficult for patrons to reach both the West and North Philadelphia Stations from Center City hotels and businesses. To make matters worse, the viaduct extending across the city was coming under increasing criticism from both officials and the public who dubbed it the "Chinese Wall" as an impediment to traffic and redevelopment of the business district west of City Hall.

The disastrous Broad Street Station fire in 1923 brought all of these problems to the forefront. Although PRR quickly cleaned up the debris and restored full operation in a matter of days, rebuilt the station platforms and tracks, and demolished the trainshed by the end of the year, it was apparent that a fresh outlook was needed to solve Philadelphia's congestion problems. Discussions between PRR and city officials began, finally resulting in the decision to located PRR's main passenger facility at 30th and Market Streets in West Philadelphia, near the site of the 1864-67 stations.

However, although this location was better suited to handle through trains than Broad Street Station, it was not ideal for commuter trains serving the city. Thus the decision was also made to separate through and commuter facilities, and to build a second station for the latter purpose. To be known as Broad Street Suburban Station (later simply Suburban Station), it was located underground beneath a new office building to be built by PRR at 16th and Arch Streets.

These two new stations became the cornerstone of a grand plan known as the Philadelphia Improvements, which called for the elimination of both West Philadelphia and Broad Street Stations along with its approach viaduct once the new facilities were completed. It also included a new main Post Office facing 30th Street Station across Market Street, a new freight and Railway Express facility to the south of that, and finally a new steam generating plant and general office building to the west of the station. Completion of this plan would allow the City of Philadelphia to carry out its Parkway program, extend Pennsylvania (now John F. Kennedy) Boulevard across the river to the station and continue West River Drive (now I-76) southward alongside the station.

The entire plan was approved by the PRR Board on June 24, 1925 and was quickly passed by the City Council a week later, which reflected the importance that city officials attached to it. However, approving and carrying out such a massive undertaking were two different things – completion would take a huge outlay of funds reach-

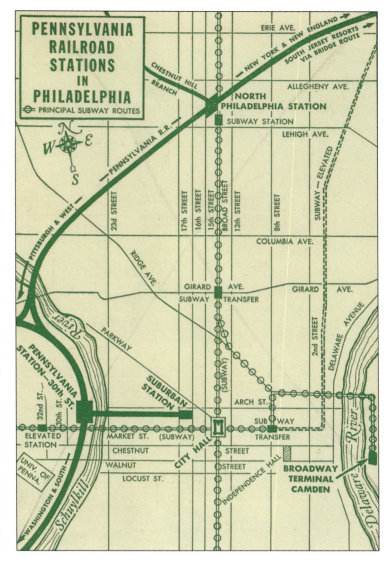

ing $85 million and much longer than the five years initially envisioned. This 1952 diagram depicts the end result, showing the relationship between 30th Street, Suburban and North Philadelphia Stations, as well as the connecting subways.

(PRR- Morning Sun Books Collection)

Implementation of the Philadelphia Improvements required close cooperation between PRR and the City. The West Philadelphia office building was completed in 1935, but construction of **Suburban Station** did not begin until 1927. The first step involved demolition of all the buildings north of the viaduct between Filbert and Cuthbert Streets from 15th Street west to the river to allow construction of the subway tunnel to Suburban Station. The distinctive 22-story office building was completed in 1929, and PRR moved its executive offices and Board Room from Broad Street Station into the upper floors and leased the rest. As shown here in a June 1985 view, the first two floors of the building are faced with polished black granite, with the upper stories in Alabama limestone and sandstone. Art Deco embellishments in ornamental cast iron and bronze provide a stunning contrast against the stonework.

The station itself opened in 1930. The waiting room was located 15' below street level, featuring marble trim and terrazzo floors, and the platform area was 20 feet below that. As built, it contained four 20 x 1130' high-level platforms serving seven tracks (an eighth was added later after the viaduct was demolished). The platform area connected via an underground concourse to Broad Street Station, City Hall and the subway system.

(William Rosenberg)

As we have noted, the plan called for Broad Street Station and the viaduct to be demolished when the other facilities were completed and then the entire available area was to be developed. PRR constructed a new stone arch bridge across the river which eventually replaced the three steel bridges, the railroad opened the north wing and the upper-level commuter platforms of 30th Street Station in 1930 and the main station for partial service in 1933, but the onset of the Depression and then World War II put further construction on hold. With both the B&O and the Reading still operating trains out of their Center City stations, PRR was reluctant to move the New York CLOCKERS and the New Jersey shore trains out of Broad Street Station.

As evidenced by this dramatic shot taken in May 1947, PRR continued not only to use Broad Street Station after World War II. Here E5s #6538 and E6s companion, both in nearly spit-and polish condition, team up to move an "Off the Beaten Track" excursion (seen later in the day on page 101 of Volume 2 at Jamesburg, N.J.) out of the venerable, but increasingly dingy station. Suburban Station is at the left, and City Hall looms above the smoke. *(David Cope)*

When 30th Street Station opened for through service in 1933, only two lower-level platforms were in operation for north-south trains. Additional platforms and tracks were opened in 1937, but further expansion was delayed until after World War II. Work finally resumed in 1950 to expand the station and the approach trackage to its planned 10-track capacity. This three-year program involved an expenditure of over $11 million, plus another $3 million to expand the trackage in Suburban Station.

This rather modest flyer announced the designation of 30th Street Station as PRR's principal downtown passenger facility, and that Broad Street Station would be closed, effective 2:01 a.m. on Sunday, April 27, 1952. The last train out of "Old Broad," #431, departed at 1:10 a.m., appropriately behind GG1 #4800, after a platform concert by the Philadelphia Orchestra and a misty-eyed singing of "Auld Lang Syne." Broad Street Station had served Philadelphia travelers for 71 years, but it had outlived its usefulness.

(PRR- Morning Sun Books Collection)

PENNSYLVANIA STATION—30TH STREET BECOMES PRINCIPAL DOWNTOWN PASSENGER STATION

PROGRESS on the Philadelphia Improvement Program and Pennsylvania Railroad Terminal Improvements permit us to make important changes both in station stops and schedules of all passenger trains now originating or terminating at Broad Street Station, Philadelphia, beginning 2:01 AM, Sunday, April 27, 1952.

Broad Street Station will be closed. Pennsylvania Station—30th Street becomes the principal downtown passenger station in Philadelphia. Extensive changes and improvements have been made—including improved lighting, new car-level platforms and additional moving stairways—for your greater convenience and comfort.

Following this action, Broad Street Station will be razed, and the area now occupied by the Station and the "Chinese Wall" will be available for an extensive mid-city development and modernization plan.

PLEASE READ THE FOLLOWING INFORMATION CAREFULLY, ESPECIALLY IF YOU HAVE BEEN ACCUSTOMED TO BOARDING OR LEAVING TRAINS AT BROAD STREET OR AT PENNSYLVANIA STATION—30TH STREET, PHILADELPHIA.

TRANSFER BETWEEN STATIONS—*Regular Suburban Trains are available for transfer between Pennsylvania Station—30th Street and Suburban Station.*

TRAIN STOPS—PENNSYLVANIA STATION—30TH STREET

The following trains will operate into or out of Pennsylvania Station—30th Street effective 2:01 A.M., Sunday, April 27:

LOWER LEVEL STATION TRACKS

PHILADELPHIA-NEW YORK hourly "clocker" trains.
NEW YORK-WASHINGTON hourly trains (as at present).
PHILADELPHIA-WASHINGTON trains.
PHILADELPHIA-BOSTON trains.
PHILADELPHIA-HARRISBURG-PITTSBURGH-ERIE-BUFFALO trains
   (Train No. 25 which carries a New York-Buffalo coach will continue to operate from New York via North Philadelphia Station.)
PHILADELPHIA-TRENTON-NEW YORK local trains except those listed on opposite page.
PHILADELPHIA-WILLIAMSPORT trains
   including outbound trains No. 527 and No. 525 Paoli-Harrisburg-Williamsport.
PHILADELPHIA-CAPE CHARLES trains.
PHILADELPHIA-ATLANTIC CITY outbound trains.
   Inbound Atlantic City-Philadelphia trains will terminate on Upper Level Tracks.
PHILADELPHIA-BALTIMORE trains.
SLEEPING CARS parked for occupancy.

UPPER LEVEL STATION TRACKS

Suburban trains serving the following lines which terminate or originate at Suburban Station will continue to use Upper Level Tracks:

PHILADELPHIA-PAOLI
   including Philadelphia-Paoli-Parkesburg outbound daily except Sunday train No. 609, daily except Saturday and Sunday train No. 621 and Sat. only trains Nos. 617 and 625. Inbound daily except Sunday trains Nos. 606 and 610, and daily except Saturday and Sunday train No. 622.
   Philadelphia-Paoli-Lancaster outbound daily except Sunday train No. 605 and inbound daily except Sunday train No. 618.

PHILADELPHIA-WILMINGTON
   except outbound train No. 421 and inbound train No. 406—which will use Lower Level Tracks.

PHILADELPHIA-WEST CHESTER
PHILADELPHIA-CHESTNUT HILL
PHILADELPHIA-NORRISTOWN

The following PHILADELPHIA-NEW YORK and PHILADELPHIA-TRENTON local trains will use Upper Level Tracks:

Northbound — Eastern Standard Time

Train No.	Frequency	Lv. Phila. Suburban Station	Lv. Phila. Pa. Sta. -30th St.	Ar. Trenton	Ar. N.Y.
252	Ex. Sat. & Sun.	4:45 AM	4:48 AM	5:40 AM	*7:23 AM
250	Sat.	4:50 AM	4:53 AM	5:44 AM	7:28 AM
3850	Ex. Sun.	6:08 AM	6:11 AM	7:02 AM	—
260	Daily	11:01 AM	11:06 AM	11:58 AM	1:42 PM
262	Sat.	12:21 PM	12:24 PM	1:20 PM	3:15 PM
276	Sat.	2:57 PM	3:01 PM	4:04 PM	5:55 PM
266	Ex. Sat. & Sun.	3:15 PM	3:18 PM	4:27 PM	6:25 PM
268	Ex. Sun.	4:16 PM	4:19 PM	5:23 PM	7:20 PM
3852	Ex. Sat. & Sun.	5:25 PM	5:28 PM	6:21 PM	

*Arrives Jersey City

Southbound

Train No.	Frequency	Lv. N.Y.	Lv. Trenton	Ar. Phila. Pa. Sta. -30th St.	Ar. Phila. Suburban Station
253	Ex. Sun.	4:05 AM	6:08 AM	7:15 AM	7:18 AM
3853	Ex. Sat. & Sun.	—	6:37 AM	7:32 AM	7:35 AM
255	Ex. Sun.	5:50 AM	7:16 AM	8:02 AM	8:05 AM
281	Sun.	6:50 AM	8:31 AM	9:18 AM	9:21 AM
3855	Ex. Sun.	—	11:06 AM	12:01 PM	12:04 PM
283	Sun.	3:55 PM	5:35 PM	6:23 PM	6:26 PM
265	Ex. Sun.	6:35 PM	8:37 PM	9:30 PM	9:33 PM

ALL TRAINS NOW USING THE NORTH PHILADELPHIA STATION WILL CONTINUE TO USE THAT STATION.

HANDLING YOUR BAGGAGE—Baggage checking and storage facilities formerly available at Broad Street Station will be transferred to Pennsylvania Station—30th Street. Telephone number for baggage information will remain EV 2-1000. Baggage will not be handled at Suburban Station.

TICKETS AND RESERVATIONS—Ticket office facilities are being expanded at Pennsylvania Station—30th Street and Suburban Station. Added personnel will be available to handle your requests for tickets, reservations, information and travel guidance. An enlarged Information Bureau will be located in the center of the Waiting Room and will be used for the Pullman "Check-in" Desk for Sleeping Car passengers.
For reservations and information continue to call EV 2-3030.

Please consult New Time Tables, effective April 27, which will be available a few days in advance.
Map showing Philadelphia stations and subway connections to Broadway Terminal, Camden, is shown on back page of this folder.

This view shows the majestic appearance of **30th Street Station** in a softly-lit 1980 image, enhancing the Alabama limestone exterior. The main west façade fronts nearly 640' on 30th Street and extends eastward almost 330' along Market Street at right. The winning design, resembling a classic temple, was developed by Graham, Anderson, Probst & White and selected from over 130 entries, including one featuring a high-rise tower.
(Morning Sun Books Collection)

The matching east façade is shown here on April 6, 1974 facing the rain-swollen Schuylkill River. The river channel was moved to the east during construction to accommodate the station and the extension of West River Drive, and it was necessary to drive some 5,000 concrete-filled steel piles to bedrock in order to obtain a secure footing in the soft silt along the riverbed. Market Street crosses the river on a graceful stone arch bridge, while I-76 the Schuylkill Expressway runs on the lower level along the river. The northeast corner of the main Post Office is visible at left. *(Al Holtz)*

The gleaming west façade shows the massive 71' high Corinthian columns that dominate the 116' high porticoes at either end of the 135x290' main concourse. This view was taken from the upper level suburban platform that serves inbound tracks 1 and 2 in September 1958. *(Will Coxey, West Jersey Chapter NRHS Collection)*

The main concourse is shown here as it appeared on October 15, 2000, after completion of a $75 million restoration to its full glory in 1988-91. The 18' long lighting fixtures are suspended from a decorative coffered ceiling 95' above the Tennessee marble floor. This view looks at the west entrance, with shops and restaurants located along the south side at left and the 60x145' main waiting room and ticket offices in the background at right. In the far corner is the entrance to the upper-level suburban wing and in the right foreground stairways descend to the through platforms on the lower level.

(Dave McKay, Morning Sun Books Collection)

The northbound SILVER METEOR led by Penn Central GG1 #4927 pulls out of 30th Street Station in June 1969. This all-reserved seat coach and sleeping car train provided service to and from Florida via Virginia, the Carolinas, Georgia and Alabama. *(William J. Brennan)*

Here's a panoramic look at the north side of the station complex taken in August 1967. The tracks at left lead into the lower level platforms for north-south trains (CLOCKERS and PRSL trains terminated here). In the center is the Race Street engine facility shown on page 19, with the upper-level suburban platforms above. These latter tracks extend eastward through the station and across the river into Suburban Station. *(William Rosenberg)*

Moving up on the suburban platforms we find Train #323, a classic Paoli local headed westward in September 1958. There are three high-level platforms serving the six tracks through the upper level.
(Will Coxey, West Jersey Chapter NRHS Collection)

A string of MP54's makes a colorful display in mixed Penn Central and newly-repainted SEPTA schemes as it traverses **Bridge 0.76** over the Schuylkill River linking the upper level of 30th Street Station with the approach to Suburban Station in September 1979. Trains must ascend a 2.2 per cent grade westward out of Suburban Station to reach this point, one of the most heavily-traveled sections of trackage in the U. S. *(William Rosenberg)*

Silverliner #213 on the suburban tracks approaches the upper level of 30th Street Station on the suburban tracks from the west in December 1967. At the left is the Philadelphia General Office Building, which was completed in 1935 as the first step of the Philadelphia Improvements. It was later sold to a private company. Also in the background is the Railway Express Agency facility relocated from just west of Broad Street Station.

To the northwest are the westward approach tracks at the far left in this March 1969 view. The approach tracks for suburban trains from the south (Wilmington and Media/West Chester) pass under the westward tracks and swing into the center upper level platform. This alignment was originally constructed in 1882 to allow PW&B trains to enter Broad Street Station. At the right, strings of MP54's occupy the **MU Storage Yard**. *(Both- William Rosenberg)*

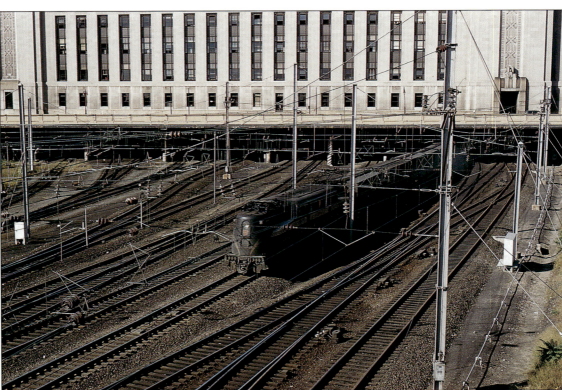

The yard and station tracks pass under the Philadelphia **General Post Office** building located south of the station and then converge into the main line southward. The massive Art Deco architectural style facility, constructed of limestone to complement the station, was completed in 1935. Here GG1 #4974 leads a string of mail and express cars out from under the complex in September 1957. *(David Cope)*

This view gives us a dramatic ground level view of the Post Office and two interesting pieces of MU equipment: RPO #5264 Class MBM62T – one of only four such cars, and a motorized combine, move southward in September 1958 in the waning months of MU RPO service in Philadelphia. These cars will move south to Arsenal Tower and then return on the southern approach tracks to Suburban Station, forming part of a local train headed to New York.

(Will Coxey, West Jersey Chapter NRHS Collection)

MAIN LINE

PHILADELPHIA TO BELLEVUE, DELAWARE

HISTORICAL BACKGROUND

The PRR main line south of Philadelphia – and its facilities – arose from a completely different background than those to the north and west of the city. However, in many ways its development was similar in terms of the relationships with road and canal building in the late 18th and early 19th Century and subsequent rail-water routes. The end result of these early efforts culminated in the formation of the Philadelphia, Wilmington & Baltimore Railroad in February 1838, which was a consolidation of three companies chartered in Pennsylvania, Delaware and Maryland to build an all-rail line between Philadelphia and Baltimore. The fourth piece of the route was the Southwark Railroad, which ran from the Schuylkill River crossing at Gray's Ferry along city streets, connecting with the city trackage and extending eastward to the docks along the Delaware River. Laid out by none other than John Edgar Thomson, this line was completed in 1835. The section of the mainline between Gray's Ferry and Wilmington was completed three years later.

The PW&B set about to upgrade the line, rebuilding bridges, improving the roadbed and replacing the strap iron rail on longitudinal stringers with 62-lb. T-section rail on wood crossties. In 1851 Samuel Morse Felton became president of the PW&B, marking the beginning of major improvements to the line. The track was re-laid with heavier T-section rail, which allowed the purchase of heavier locomotives to handle the increased traffic. Many older frame passenger stations along the line were replaced with new brick structures, and a new passenger and freight terminal was opened at Broad and Prime Streets, which was the largest such facility in the city at the time. To accommodate heavy Civil War traffic the PW&B launched a program to double-track the line in 1863, which was essentially completed in 1866.

Under Felton's successor, Isaac Hinckley, the decision was made in 1869 to replace the iron rail with steel, a program that was completed in the late 1870s. In 1870 the PW&B began a project known as the Darby Improvements to relocate the main line between Gray's Ferry and Chester farther to the west, away from the frequent flooding in the low-lying terrain along the Delaware River. This was completed in 1872, and in the following year the old line was leased to the Reading for use as a freight branch. In conjunction with the new double-tracked line the PW&B actively promoted several upscale suburban communities to compete with PRR's highly-successful Main Line development west of the city.

With these improvements completed by the late 1870s, the PW&B was ranked with the best railroads in the U.S. It had a double-track, all-steel rail, stone-ballasted mainline connecting Philadelphia and Baltimore, in addition to control of several branches including the West Chester & Philadelphia and the Philadelphia & Baltimore Central from Philadelphia to Octoraro Junction with the Columbia & Port Deposit Railroad along the Susquehanna River. It enjoyed steadily increasing traffic, both freight and passenger, and the prosperity it brought. However, things were about to change.

In 1862 under pressure from the Union Army, the PW&B had entered into a joint agreement with PRR and the Reading to build the Junction Railroad, which provided an all-rail route through the city in the following year to replace the arduous and time-consuming rail-water route via the Camden & Amboy. There were still delays as a direct route had to wait for the completion of the southern portion of the Junction Railroad in 1866 and the Connecting Railway, which was finally opened in 1867.

With Thomson's acquisition of the key Baltimore & Potomac Railroad in 1867 and the lease of the United New Jersey Railroad and Canal Company in 1871, PRR was in a strategic position to secure an all-rail route between New York City and Washington, DC by obtaining control of the PW&B, the critical link between the two. PRR had purchased the Reading's share of the Junction Railroad in 1879, and then leased it to the PW&B. However, there was one obstacle: The Baltimore & Ohio Railroad, under the contentious and often erratic leadership of John W. Garrett. After launching a brief rate war with PRR in 1874, Garrett in 1880 suddenly transferred through B&O traffic from the UNJRR routing to the Reading's newly-acquired trackage rights on the CNJ to reach New York markets.

In retaliation PRR imposed an extra charge and insisted on utilizing its own locomotives to move B&O traffic on the Junction Railroad through Philadelphia. The B&O obtained a Federal court order to put an end to such practices, but delays persisted. Garrett then made a high-stakes attempt to secure control of PW&B stock – and lost. PRR emerged as the winner and in July 1881 completed the purchase for $15 million, taking over operation of the line on October 31. Thus, in just 14 years, PRR had put together a direct all-rail route between New York City and the nation's capital, and the B&O had to build its own line to Philadelphia to connect with the Reading.

PRR implemented a major program to further upgrade the line, including heavier steel rail, several passing sidings as well as new iron bridges, all to facilitate heavier traffic flow. In 1902 PRR consolidated the PW&B and the B&P, forming the Philadelphia, Baltimore and Washington Railroad, which continued to be operated as a separate company under PRR control. Further upgrading of the line took place under the 1902 Improvements program, notably elevation of the right-of-way through Chester and other urban areas. Like similar programs on the New York Division, this involved elevating the trackbed on fill supported by heavy masonry retaining walls and plate girder bridges over city streets. However, unlike the New York Division, third and fourth tracks were added only when and where needed. Finally the PW&B was fully integrated into PRR on January 1, 1918 under a 999-year lease, signaling the end of an era.

Interlocking	Interlocking Station	Block Station	MAIN LINE	Distance from
X	X	X-O	ARSENAL	2
X	X	X-O	BRILL	4
			DARBY	6
			CURTIS PARK	7
			SHARON HILL	7
			COLCROFT	8
			GLENOLDEN	8
			NORWOOD	9
			MOORE	9
			RIDLEY PARK	10
			CRUM LYNNE	11
X	X	X	BALDWIN	11
			EDDYSTONE	12
X	X	X	CHESTER	13
			LAMOKIN	14
			LAMOKIN ST.	14
			HIGHLAND AVE.	15
X	X	X	TRAINER	16
			HOOK	16
			MARCUS HOOK	17
			NAAMAN	18
			CLAYMONT	19
			HOLLY OAK	21
			BELLEVUE	22
			DIVISION POST (Ches. Div.)	22

Arsenal Tower (MP 2.1 from Suburban Station) is located at the southern end of the Philadelphia Terminal area. It was named after the U. S. Government Arsenal formerly located on the east side of the Schuylkill River. The tower's original function was to control the crossing of the Delaware Extension and the PW&B mainline at grade. However, with the 1902 Improvements a new tower was built with a greatly expanded role as the southern counterpart to Zoo Tower. This was in turn replaced in 1932 with this building containing a 99-lever electro-pneumatic machine for north-south traffic on the main, suburban traffic to and from the West Chester Branch as well as freight traffic on and off the High Line and the Delaware Extension. This northward view of the three-story brick tower was made on July 22, 1972 – just visible at right is the southern approach to the High Line. *(John P. Stroup)*

Our photographer captured a southbound Amtrak train in June 1981 with an interesting power lashup pulling a long string of Amfleet coaches: GG1 #4877 newly resplendent in PRR Tuscan Red and Gold, GG1 #4876 in Conrail/Amtrak stealth black and F40PH #363 celebrate the GG1's role in service on PRR. The train is stopped in front of the tower on southward main Track #4; to the right is northward main Track #1. At extreme left are tracks to the West Chester Branch and in the center is the track leading to the South Street Yard. The building at the left is the Philadelphia Civic Center.
(Harold A. Smith)

Brill Tower (MP 4.2) is the second mainline tower south of the city serving the Philadelphia Division. It controlled a complete set of crossovers on the four-track mainline separating 30th Street and Suburban Stations passenger trains in addition to routing freights to and from the High Line. Here a long string of northbound Penn Central MP54's rolls past the tower in August 1974. *(William Rosenberg)*

Brill Tower's 40-lever mechanical machine was a museum piece by the time of this December 1980 record.
(Dave Cope)

Three photos illustrate suburban service on the main line south of Philadelphia and the rudimentary shelters which replaced traditional PRR station buildings. In the first, taken on August 23, 1982 a pair of Silverliner IV's rolls past the boarded up brick shelter at **Darby** (MP 6.1), the first station stop on this section of the line. The lead unit bears both Penn Central and the original SEPTA logo. Darby was originally settled by Quakers along the namesake creek around 1660 and was incorporated as a borough in 1852. *(Harold A. Smith)*

Curtis Park (MP 6.8) is a station stop in Darby Township, located about half-way between Darby and Folcroft. On March 30, 1968 southbound Train #913 consisting of Silverliner III's #224 and 234 pauses at the station, which has a small single-story waiting room on the northbound side and unusual cantilevered steel platform sheds.
(William M. Tilden)

Folcroft (MP 7.7) has had an interesting history, both as a manufacturing and residential area. It was originally part of a land grant from William Penn that became a large farm owned by John Knowles. The property passed through several owners, finally ending up in the hands of the H.K. Mulford Company, which named it Warwick. H. K. Mulford, an early manufacturing chemical company with offices in New York, Chicago and Philadelphia, expanded their property holdings for grazing land for livestock used in the production of smallpox and diphtheria vaccines. By 1957 the Barrett Division of Allied Chemical & Dye Co. had taken over much of the site for the manufacture of coal tar products.

Folcroft, which means "leafy field" in Old English, was first used by PRR in the early 1880s to promote development of one of the early suburban communities along the PW&B. The railroad constructed a two-story frame station on the northbound side of the tracks subsequently replaced with a Type 2B-3 and a shelter on the opposite side. The right-of-way was four-tracked by the 1890s with the center two tracks used primarily for freight. By November 23, 1982 with greatly diminished freight traffic on the Northeast Corridor, the center tracks are used by Amtrak, while SEPTA mainly uses the outside tracks for their frequently stopping locals. Here Silverliner IV #340 heads southward past the Folcroft shelter. *(Harold A. Smith)*

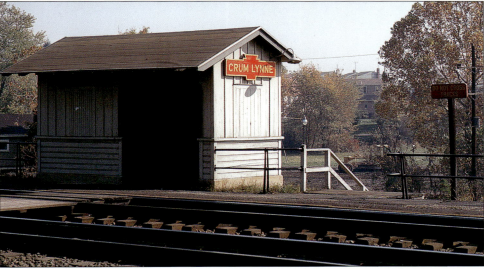

Next are two images made in November 1968 of stations serving suburban commuters established by the PW&B. **Glenolden** (MP 8.3), originally known as Warwick Annex, was also part of the Knowles Farm property. Later it was selected as the site of a large park laid out by the PW&B to allow Philadelphia residents to escape the heat of the city during the summer. The one-story stone station, nearly identical to the one in Sharon Hill to the north, was built in the 1880s on the southbound side, where a group of youngsters step onto the tracks without paying much attention to the potential danger.

The **Crum Lynne** (MP 11.1) station is located at the southern end of Ridley Park, the largest and most elegant of the planned suburban communities in the 1870s by the PW&B. The development featured the 50-room Ridley Park Hotel overlooking landscaped vistas including man-made lakes and streams. Here a small frame shelter serves commuters in the area.

Baldwin Tower (MP 11.7) is located near the long-closed Eddystone plant of the famed Baldwin Locomotive Works, builder of legions of steam and diesel locomotives for PRR and many other roads. The two-story concrete base structure, shown here in September 1980 with wood sheathing over the upper portion, housed an electro-pneumatic machine that controlled crossovers on the mainline and industrial sidings that once served the locomotive works and the Pittsburgh Mill Steel Company located on the west side of the tracks.
(All- Emery Gulash, Morning Sun Books Collection)

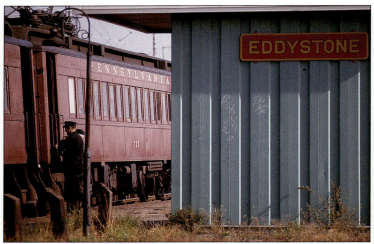 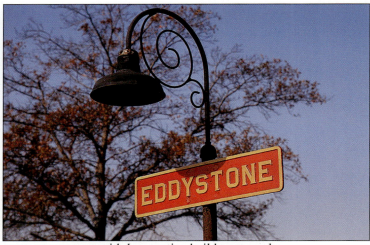

Eddystone (MP 12.3) is among a handful of town names synonymous with locomotive builders, namely, La Grange, Schenectady, Beloit, Lima and Eddystone. In November 1966, the goose-neck lamp and MP54 are reminders that the town once had a station more befitting its stature in American railroading.
(Both- Emery Gulash, Morning Sun Books Collection)

Chester (MP 13.4), originally called Upland, was initially intended to be the seat of government of William Penn's proprietary colony. However, when he took possession in 1682, the location was changed to upriver in Philadelphia. Chester instead developed into a center for shipbuilding on the riverfront and the location of cotton and woolen mills along Chester Creek.

The first railroad station was a modest two-story frame structure built in 1837 that also served as the residence for the agent. This structure was replaced by the PW&B in 1854 with a larger one-story brick building, which served passengers until the 1903 Improvements that resulted in a new station being constructed alongside the elevated four-track right-of-way. The attractive two-story brick structure shown here on October 26, 1974 was located on the northbound side. Similar to those built at about the same time in New Brunswick and Elizabeth, New Jersey, on the New York Division, the first floor housed the ticket office and baggage room, with the main waiting room located on the second floor at track level. The second view captures north- and southbound suburban trains stopping at the station on the same date during the Penn Central era. *(Both- Harold A. Smith)*

Marcus Hook takes its name from the major Lenni Lenape Indian settlement located there that subsequently became a Swedish trading post in the 1640s. Early shipbuilding industry developed along the riverfront, and in later years it became the site of a massive array of industrial plants, especially oil refineries that were accessed by the PRR South Chester Branch and served by Thurlow Yard.

Hook Tower (MP 16.8) was located at the southern end of this complex and controlled the crossovers on the mainline as well as the junction with the industrial trackage. In this northward view made on April 11, 1975, the siding applied to the upper story of the two-story brick tower stands in sharp contrast to the grimy MP54's – one red and one green, perhaps symbolizing the failed Penn Central merger.

(James P. Shuman)

The right-of-way in the area between Holly Oak and Bellevue, Delaware runs very close to the Delaware River as evidenced in this view of Amtrak GG1 #913 leading a train northbound on April 11, 1975. There are many small streams that drain into the river through the area, necessitating culverts typical of the ones shown here, an example of unheralded but very necessary facilities. Our money is on the train reaching Philadelphia well ahead of the tug making its way upriver with a barge. The Division Post with the Chesapeake Division is close by at MP 22.3. *(James P. Shuman)*

While looking at smaller facilities like culverts, here are three more shown in August 1967. The first is a perfect example of a classic PRR **Standard Passenger Shelter**, a "Design "B" or Type W-35 Wood Frame Shelter Shed for "unimportant stations." The location is unknown, but it doesn't matter – there were untold numbers everywhere along the line, supplementing the larger station facilities. As described in the PRR Standard Plans, the shelter rests on a platform, is sheathed on the inside of the frame with white pine boards and the roof is supported with simple uncarved brackets. This shed was originally equipped with a plank bench, but it has been replaced with a decidedly non-standard chair brought from parts unknown.

The second example gives us another classic, albeit a less common one, a PRR **Standard Concrete Watch Box**. The entire structure was made of reinforced concrete, including 3" thick walls, floor and roof, the latter molded with red cement to represent tile. The smoke jack is also concrete, as is the molded keystone. The interior was equipped with a wooden sloping wall desk, bench and small locker. The ravages of time and perhaps vandalism have taken their toll on the small structure seen serving here as "K" Block Limit station in Hightstown, N.J.

And finally, to complete the north-south main line portion of this volume (we will look at branches first and then return to the main), we present a PRR **Standard Whistle Sign**. According to the 1927 standard, the dimensions of the keystone are 16" high and wide, and "letters and borders shall be raised 1/8th inch with slight draft. All parts of the sign shall be painted black except the background which shall be white." The sign will be positioned not less than 8' from the gauge line of the (outer) rail and "Except where regulated by local ordinances or other laws the prescribed sign shall be located at a distance of not less than 1200' nor more than 1650' in advance of the grade road crossing or point for which the warning is to be sounded."

(All- William Rosenberg)

CHESTNUT HILL BRANCH

			CHESTNUT HILL BRANCH	*
X	X	X-O	NORTH PHILADELPHIA	
			WESTMORELAND	0.8
			QUEEN LANE	2.2
			CHELTEN AVENUE	2.8
			TULPEHOCKEN	3.3
			UPSAL	3.8
			CARPENTER	4.4
			ALLEN LANE	4.8
			ST. MARTINS	5.6
			HIGHLAND	6.1
X	B	B	CHESTNUT HILL	6.6

HISTORICAL BACKGROUND

The Chestnut Hill Branch was constructed by PRR in 1883-04 as the Philadelphia, Germantown & Chestnut Hill Railroad, in direct competition with the Reading Company's line located farther to the east to that growing upscale residential suburb. The 6.5-mile long, double-track line was well-constructed. It cost some $2 million to build largely because of the cuts through the hard Wissahickon Schist and fills in the hilly terrain. It was a fine example of a railroad built to serve PRR-sponsored real estate development of upscale communities that would in turn generate business for the railroad.

The lower end of the line became industrialized, with the short Midvale Branch serving the Midvale Steel Company and later the Budd Company. However, most of the line is suburban, traversing the rugged Wissahickon Creek Valley along the edge of Philadelphia's Fairmount Park. The branch was electrified in 1918.

At one time the Fort Washington Branch extended from Cresheim Junction located between Allen Lane and St. Martins to White Marsh on the Trenton Cutoff. The Fort Washington Branch was electrified in 1924. Passenger service on this single-track line was generally light with most of the station stops having small shelters or even just platforms. For a time there were six to eight trains daily in each direction, including through operations from Broad Street Station to Trenton via the Cutoff.

The Chestnut Hill Branch begins at the junction with the main at **North Philadelphia**, controlled by the tower of the same name. The shelters and platforms serving the branch are located on a tight curve at the west end of the main station platform. The heavy, concrete-enclosed girder bridges at left carry both the branch (#0.06) and the main (#84.69) over the Reading mainline into Philadelphia. Southbound (railroad westward) Silverliner III #263 pauses at the shelter in May 1970. *(William Rosenberg)*

In 1918 PRR undertook a project to eliminate most of the grade crossings on the line in conjunction with the electrification, primarily by placing the right-of-way in cuts. The end result is clearly evident in this view of the depressed track grade through the **Chelten Avenue** station (MP 2.8). The original two-story brick station, built at street level in 1886 and rebuilt in 1915, is just visible at right in this July 19, 1969 view. *(Harold A. Smith)*

PRR commissioned noted Philadelphia architect W. Bleddyn Powell who was responsible for the original Broad Street Station and the completion of Philadelphia's City Hall to design most of the stations on the Chestnut Hill Branch so that the upscale clientele would feel right at home. The one at **Tulpehocken** (MP 3.3), (its name stems from a Lenape Indian word meaning "land of turtles") is typical – a stately two-story brick structure with multiple dormers. A pair of southbound Silverliners approaches the station on June 11, 1966. *(James P. Shuman)*

Originally a one-story Type B-2, like several other stations on the line it had a second story added in 1889-90 to provide spacious quarters for the agent. Typically the main waiting room and ticket office was located on one side of the right-of-way with a matching shelter on the other, as shown here at Tulpehocken in a February 1982 view. The SEPTA engineer eyes the photographer warily. *(Harold A. Smith)*

Allen Lane station (MP 4.8), located in the Mount Airy section of Philadelphia, derived its name from William Allen, a prominent colonial era citizen whose estate gave the neighborhood its name. Southbound Silverliner III #239 and colleague pause at the trackside shelter on September 25, 1976. The stairs at right lead to the main two-story brick station located at street level, just visible at upper right. At one time the station housed Allen Lane Tower, which controlled the junction and power to the Fort Washington Branch (later the Fort Washington Yard Running Track), just to the north. The humpback bridge in the background was built in 1910 to allow passengers to safely access the southbound platform. *(Harold A. Smith)*

St. Martins (MP 5.6) has been known for decades as the best maintained and most attractively landscaped station on the branch, as amply demonstrated here in a September 1963 view. The two-story brick structure, built in 1887, is located on the southbound side, barely visible at the left. This view also gives us a look at newly-delivered Silverliner II #259, part of an order of 38 cars delivered to PRR along with the Reading in that year to replace aging MU cars on both roads. The brilliant red geraniums complement the PRR keystone logo. *(William Rosenberg)*

Chestnut Hill was originally part of Germantown Township and served as a gateway between Philadelphia and the surrounding towns and farmlands. The village initially served as a summer vacation spot for city residents because of its high elevation and cooler temperatures, later becoming part of the City of Philadelphia in 1854 under the Act of Consolidation. In the latter part of the 19th Century it grew to become an affluent residential community served by streetcars and two rail lines, allowing easy commuting to Center City.

Austin Tower controlled the movements at the entrance to the PRR terminal area, where a small yard was located at one time south of the passenger station. This July 1969 view looks southward on the branch.

Chestnut Hill station (MP 6.6) was constructed in 1886 at the terminus of the branch, located just off Germantown Avenue. As built, the attractive two-story brick structure had a prominent center gable and spire. These were later removed, but the expansive canopy surrounding the building on all four sides is still intact in this July 1969 view. We suspect that the Rambler with New Jersey plates in the foreground belonged to our photographer. *(Both- John Dziobko, Jr.)*

The tracks are nestled between the station and a small ridge, as shown here in a February 16, 1981 view. The designation "Chestnut Hill West" was coined by SEPTA to distinguish this station and line from that of the former Reading Company to the east. *(Harold A. Smith)*

PRR constructed this open frame shed at street level along Germantown Avenue (Route 422), the main thoroughfare through town. Featuring a newsstand, telephone booth, soda machine and a small bench for connecting bus passengers, it allowed convenient access to the main station via the stairway at left. We will leave it to the reader to decide if the latter day color scheme enhances or detracts from the Victorian turned support posts, curved roof brackets and gingerbread trim. Meanwhile SEPTA made an effort to attract riders by advertising a 35-cent fare to Center City in July 1969.
(John Dziobko, Jr. and William Rosenberg)

WEST CHESTER BRANCH

Interlocking	Interlocking Station	Block Station	WEST CHESTER BRANCH	*Distance from
X	X	X-O	ARSENAL...............	2
			FORTY-NINTH STREET.......	3
			ANGORA...............	4
			FERNWOOD-YEADON........	5
			LANSDOWNE.............	6
			GLADSTONE.............	6
			CLIFTON-ALDAN..........	7
			PRIMOS................	8
			SECANE................	9
			MORTON-RUTLEDGE.......	10
			SWARTHMORE...........	11
			WALLINGFORD...........	12
			MOYLAN-ROSE VALLEY.....	13
X	X		MEDIA................	14
			ELWYN................	15
			WILLIAMSON SCHOOL.....	15
			GLEN RIDDLE...........	16
			LENNI................	17
			WAWA................	18
			DARLINGTON...........	18
			GLEN MILLS............	20
			LOCKSLEY..............	21
			CHEYNEY..............	22
			WESTTOWN............	23
			END OF BLOCK SIGN.....	26
			NIELDS ST.............	27
			WEST CHESTER.........	27

HISTORICAL BACKGROUND

The rail connection between Philadelphia and West Chester has had a fascinating history. In fact, for a time there were two competing railroads, each vying for traffic and financing. It all began back in 1831 with the chartering of the pioneering West Chester Railroad, which ran northward out of its namesake town a short distance to connect with the Philadelphia & Columbia Railroad then under construction. It opened in 1832, joining the P&C at what was then known as West Chester Intersection, now Malvern. The relationship with the P&C was initially friendly; in fact the P&C provided locomotives for the WCRR, which located its terminal on Broad Street in Philadelphia. This was later moved to Market Street near 18th Street when the P&C changed its route into the city.

However the WCRR shortly ran into difficulties. It was forced to pay high tolls to operate over the P&C and experienced constant operating delays over the increasingly uncooperative state road. Calls from prominent West Chester citizens for a new line directly into the city resulted in the chartering of the West Chester & Philadelphia Railroad in 1848, but this road had difficulty raising funds and encountered additional delays during construction because of the hilly terrain and the need to build bridges over several streams. The line was completed from Philadelphia to Media in 1854, and finally reached West Chester in 1858. This road established a freight depot in the city at the corner of Market and 18th Streets near the WCRR facility and a passenger terminal and engine service facility at 31st and Chestnut in West Philadelphia, which was expanded several times over the years.

Meanwhile PRR had taken over the P&C and in 1859 assumed operation of the WCRR, later extending the line to Frazer that became the new junction with the east-west main. An unbelievably complex series of financial moves and court battles ensued over the next several years. The end result was that both the WCRR and the WC&P came under PRR control in 1881, to be operated as part of the PW&B. In the following year trains were shifted from the terminal at 31st and Chestnut into newly-completed Broad Street Station, using the Junction Railroad to access the bridge across the Schuylkill River. The former WC&P depot was converted for freight service except for a brief return when Broad Street Station was being enlarged in 1893.

Under PRR auspices the PW&B launched a program to upgrade the branch. The line was double-tracked beginning in 1882, and several substantial new brick stations were constructed. With the building of new steel bridges across the major streams, this program was finally completed as far as Elwyn in 1896. The line via Frazer was subsequently abandoned.

After its heyday as part of the line to Octoraro Junction, traffic on the West Chester branch declined sharply after World War II as a result of highway competition from automobiles, trucks and buses. PRR discontinued through passenger service to West Chester in 1948, with passengers required to change trains to a shuttle at Media. SEPTA restored service on an upgraded right-of-way in 1983, but buses were substituted for trains south of Elwyn in 1986.

The first stop is at **Fernwood-Yeadon** (MP 5.4), shown in these September 1980 views. In the first photo a trio of Silverliner IV's pauses at the station serving the two communities. If we overlook the ad posters and rampant graffiti in the second image, we find a small gem. Possibly the remnant of a longer structure, a frame shelter shed open on the platform side is attached to an enclosed shed with a gable showing elaborate carved fretwork on the front. At one time the junction with the lightly-traveled Newtown Square Branch was a short distance beyond this location. This line was cut back to Grassland in 1963 and the remainder abandoned in 1982. *(Both- Harold A. Smith)*

Lansdowne (MP 6.3) was settled in the early 1700s and incorporated as a borough in 1893. It was the location of early textile mills and later several iron and steel industries after PRR laid a second track on the line. In the first November 1966 view is the attractive main station located on the northward (inbound) side. It is a single-story brick structure (similar to Type B-6, but with an offset agent's bay), built in 1901 and enlarged in 1905. It was designed by the famed Philadelphia architect Frank Furness, who was also responsible for several elegant houses in the borough. A steel frame shed (similar to Type S-33) runs along the trackside and is supported by heavy brackets secured to the main structure. It suffered the later indignity of a catenary column thrust through the roof.

A detail shot taken on the same date reveals the delicate carved fretwork under the center gable.

The southbound station is an elongated shelter shed, more typical of structures found on the Main Line to the west. Built in 1890, it is similar to Type W-35, except that there is an enclosed area along the back of the entire structure with long iron brackets supporting the roof overhand. An enclosed waiting room is located under the center gable. Note the elaborate stairway leading to street level.

(All- Emery Gulash, Morning Sun Books Collection)

Sadly, by the time of this October 23, 1974 photo the main station has become badly weatherbeaten, but nevertheless still intact as inbound Silverliner II #258 makes a stop. However, the southbound shelter has been reduced to a single section and the roadbed could use some work. Fortunately, this story has a happy ending. Faced with its demolition, a group of concerned citizens secured funds, and the main station was beautifully restored with the trackside dormer rebuilt to its original configuration in 1995.

The Form 37 West Chester Branch public timetable retained its gold color during the PRR to PC transition.
(Morning Sun Books Collection)

The attempt to continue use of the station sign while eliminating the PRR Keystone was not very subtle – in fact, quite disconcerting to true PRR fans! By the time of this October 27, 1978 photograph, the same ham-handed tack was even being practiced on the Penn Central logo on this MU. *(All- Harold A. Smith)*

Clifton-Aldan (MP 7.5) was formerly known as Clifton, the site of early 19th Century textile mills, as well as the country residence of PRR President Tom Scott. The interesting two-story stone station was constructed in 1869 on the inbound side. The outbound frame shelter (similar to Type W-36) was added in 1890. Both are in remarkably good condition in this May 5, 1992 view. *(Harold A. Smith)*

Looking in the other direction on June 22, 1971 we find another survivor, the frame freight station constructed by the PW&B in 1889 (similar to Type W-18). Building paint is a distant memory and some latter-day changes have been made, but the structure is otherwise intact.
(Richard H. Young, Morning Sun Books Collection)

The attractive brick station serving **Morton-Rutledge** (MP 9.9) was built in 1880 on property purchased from the estate of John Edgar Thomson, who maintained a summer home in the community. The town was originally known as Newton's, but was renamed Morton in the 1860s after a prominent judge who also had a mansion nearby. Here a pair of Silverliners pauses at the inbound station on September 21, 1974. The outbound shelter is identical to the one at Clifton-Aldan.
(Harold A. Smith)

A string of MP54's pauses at **Swarthmore** (MP 11.2) in April 1968, just two months into the Penn Central merger. The attractive two-story brick station just visible at left was built in 1877. The shelter sheds and extended platforms were added in 1930-31 in conjunction with a grade crossing elimination project. *(Gerald H. Landau Collection)*

By September 1975 not only was the sign repainted in Penn Central colors, but the station itself had been demolished leaving only the shelter sheds. Swarthmore was originally called West Dale after the noted 18th Century artist Benjamin West, but it was renamed in the 1870s after the nearby college established by the Quakers. A pair of newly-delivered Silverliner IV's led by #308 drops off a group of college students. *(Harold A. Smith)*

Wallingford (MP 12.7) was founded in 1776 and named by the settlers after Wallingford, England. On April 29, 1979, the Philadelphia Chapter of the NRHS had an excursion train on the branch. All eyes and cameras are focused on the string of MP54's newly-repainted in the striking SEPTA color scheme. *(William Rosenberg)*

The attractive Victorian station, serving the award-winning residential community, was designed by famed Philadelphia architect Frank Furness and built by the PW&B in the 1880s. Fortunately, it and its shelter have been lovingly preserved and were photographed on August 15, 2001.

(Both- Dr. Art Peterson)

Media (MP 14.0), the county seat of Delaware County was incorporated as a borough in 1850 and was an important stop from the early days of the WC&P, which built an attractive two-story brick station here in 1855. With growing traffic, this facility was enlarged in 1868 and again in 1881-82 after the PRR takeover to house the Central Division Superintendent's offices, which were relocated from the WC&P depot in West Philadelphia. In 1887 the double track was extended from Swarthmore to Media and the station platform area expanded, resulting in the imposing Mansard-roofed structure and track layout depicted in this circa 1907 postcard view.
(Morning Sun Books Collection)

That structure was demolished in 1951 and replaced with this decidedly unimposing flat-roofed single-story brick station shown here in a northward view in May 1975. With declining traffic, in 1953 the double track was cut back from Elwyn to just north of Media. Wawa Tower was closed and the interlocking machine relocated to the Media station. *(Will Coxey, West Jersey Chapter NRHS Collection)*

Under the track rationalization project Track #2 became the single main track to West Chester. The old southward platform was eliminated, and the island platform shown here was built to allow passengers to transfer to West Chester trains, using the stub-ended Shuttle Track. The end of Track #1 became part of the storage yard south of the station. This southward view of the station area was made from the Orange Street overpass bridge on October 7, 1980.
(Richard H. Young, Morning Sun Books Collection)

This May 26, 1957 view looks southward at the passenger station serving **Wawa** (MP 18.0), an unincorporated community in Delaware County named after the Ojibwa Indian word for "goose." The single-story brick structure was built in 1911, replacing a two-story brick station with agent's quarters constructed in 1867. It features a trapezoidal-shaped passenger shelter and a pedestrian tunnel allowing access to both the West Chester (right) and Octoraro (left) branches.

In its heyday in the late 19th Century, Wawa was a busy junction with frequent service and passengers transferring from one line to the other justifying a roundhouse and coaling wharf located nearby. Traffic subsequently declined, particularly after World War II, leading to the discontinuation of passenger service on the Octoraro Branch in 1948. The remaining freight service was provided by a Chester-based (Chesapeake Division) local. *(John Dziobko, Jr.)*

Glen Mills (MP 20.2) was the location of early textile mills along Chester Creek, resulting in a number of prosperous citizens, who built attractive homes in the community. The elegant two-story brick station serving this upscale clientele was another Frank Furness design built in 1881.

With its elaborate Victorian wood trim and detailed brickwork, the station is considered to be the most attractive on the branch. Fortunately this structure has been restored in recent years as well. The West Chester shuttle pauses at the station on a warm July day in 1973.
(William Rosenberg)

The station serving the small community of **Cheyney** has had an interesting history. The original frame passenger and freight stations were constructed by an industrious local merchant in 1867 to generate business on the line. PRR purchased the property in 1909 to build the one-story frame structure (similar to Type W-3) shown here in July 1973. The block station located here was closed in 1953 as part of a rationalization program.
(William Rosenberg)

The NRHS excursion stopped at **Westtown** (MP 23.9) as well in April 1979, but at least here we get a good look at the station. The two-story frame structure was constructed in 1881, during the station-building period following the PRR takeover. It replaced an early station built in 1858 to serve the Westtown Boarding School established by Quakers in 1799. *(Harold A. Smith)*

Westtown is the first stop in largely rural Chester County, and the resemblance of the station to a farmhouse is particularly evident in this view looking west from Penn Central Train #736 on May 3, 1975. For many years the rambling structure served not only as the station and agent's quarters, but also as the town post office and local gathering place. *(Al Holtz)*

We now reach historic **West Chester** (MP 27.4), settled by Quakers in the early 18th Century and the county seat of Chester County since 1786. The county courthouse built in the 1840s was designed in the classical revival style by Thomas Walter, one of the architects of the U.S. Capitol. The WC&P constructed a small three-stall roundhouse and turntable in the southeastern part of town when it opened in 1858 and a freight station nearby in 1867. Because of limited finances it had to swallow its independent pride and share the WCRR passenger depot for several years. Finally in 1880 it was able to construct a terminal of its own, an imposing two-story brick structure facing Market Street in the center of town. The station was still active when this view was made on August 18, 1960. *(Walter E. Zullig, Jr.)*

As built the terminal consisted of this rather ornate Italianate structure with train sheds extending back from the head house. A fire heavily damaged the station in 1885, but in typical PRR fashion repairs were quickly carried out. With declining traffic in the 20th Century, however, the station was gradually reduced in size. The train shed was razed and the remaining passenger boarding facilities reduced to one platform shelter serving two tracks. By May 1967 the main station had been closed and boarded up.
(David Cope)

And by May 1975 the building had been demolished and the shelter cut back further to this forlorn remnant.
(Will Coxey, West Jersey Chapter NRHS Collection)

WEST PHILADELPHIA ELEVATED BRANCH DELAWARE EXTENSION

			WEST PHILADELPHIA ELEVATED BRANCH
X	X	X-O	ZOO
X	X	X-O	ARSENAL
X	X	X-O	BRILL

The direction from Zoo to Brill is southward.
Trainphone locations other than Block Stations—
Train Dispatchers office.
Grays Ferry Yard office.
*Distance from Zoo.

DELAWARE EXTENSION

X	X	X-O	ARSENAL
X	X	X-O	PENROSE—R-Stadium
	X	X-O	STADIUM
X-A			PAY (B. & O. Crossing)

The direction from Arsenal to Stadium is eastward.
Trainphone locations other than Block Stations—
Train Dispatchers office.
Penrose, Greenwich, Greenwich Coal Yard, Penna. Produce Terminal, Tidewater, South Phila. Ore Yard and D-16 Yard offices.
*Distance from Arsenal.

HISTORICAL BACKGROUND

From its early days PRR recognized the importance of serving Philadelphia port facilities on the Delaware River, and in particular the need to access this area by a separate line that would eliminate the delays of moving freight through the congested city streets. A new line, known as the Delaware Extension, was constructed in 1861 from the Junction Railroad across the Schuylkill River at the Arsenal Bridge to serve a new grain elevator at the foot of Washington Avenue. This line was extended to a yard laid out at Greenwich in 1863-66. Over the next decades the port facilities all along the Delaware riverfront were enlarged, and PRR extended trackage to serve them. In 1880 PRR built a new line along the Schuylkill River to Arsenal Bridge known as the Schuylkill River Branch, to bypass the Junction Railroad and improve traffic flow in West Philadelphia, and a new deck truss bridge was constructed at Arsenal in 1885-86. The West Philadelphia Elevated Line, commonly known as the High Line, was built through West Philadelphia as part of the 1902 Improvements Program. It allowed direct access from the junction with the east-west and north-south mainlines at Zoo Tower to Arsenal Bridge leading to the Delaware Extension and Greenwich Yard. This brilliantly conceived, 2.3-mile viaduct allowed eastward freight tonnage, especially coal trains from Enola Yard, to move to the Philadelphia riverfront without having to pass through the increasingly congested area in West Philadelphia.

Finally, in 1926-28 the north-south portion of the Delaware Extension was elevated along the 25th Street Viaduct, eliminating several grade crossings in South Philadelphia. In addition, a new joint PRR-B&O line was built to the Navy Yard and eastward to a greatly-expanded South Philadelphia Terminal Yard at Greenwich Point. A new South Philadelphia Freight Terminal and Produce Yard were also constructed at this time, giving PRR expansive new freight facilities serving the Delaware Riverfront.

We return to the **High Line**, this time the middle section, in this December 1963 view from the approach to the upper level of 30th Street Station. Looking to the northwest, this view shows one of the deck truss spans supported on masonry piers as well as the plate girders on steel piers making up most of this portion of the viaduct. Behind the structure just a corner of the Passenger Service Building is visible, and beyond that is the West Philadelphia Steam Plant. This massive facility was built in 1929 as the first part of the Philadelphia Improvements to provide steam heat to both 30th Street Station and Suburban Station across the river. But it also gives us a look at something else - a long string of Silverliner II's on the normally freight-only line can only be headed to the classic Army-Navy football game. *(Gerald H. Landau)*

The second December 1963 view was made a bit farther south and gives us another look at a special train headed to the game, this time a string of heavyweight varnish behind GG1 #4931 resplendent in the single-stripe scheme. Note that both of these trains are traveling left-handed inbound on Track #1. At the left is the University of Pennsylvania Stadium, with the southern end of the Grays Ferry Branch (former Junction Railroad) just visible under the locomotive. *(Gerald H. Landau)*

The Delaware Extension crossed the Schuylkill River over **Arsenal Bridge**, so named because of the U. S. Army facility located on the east side of the river south of the bridge. The first bridge was a three-span iron through truss structure built in 1861 with the center span a pivoting draw. That bridge was replaced in 1885-86 with the structure shown here in September 1947. This nine-span deck truss is made up of a 192' draw span (bridge 1.87), three spans on the west approach totaling 320' and five on the east approach extending the same distance. This opportune view looking northward along the east bank of the river was made from a fan trip on B&O trackage as an eastbound PRR freight heads across the bridge. The coal barge is being unloaded at the Philadelphia Electric Company Schuylkill Generating Station located to the north of the bridge which provided electricity for the Main Line into Broad Street Station. In the distance is the Philadelphia General Post Office on the west bank of the river.

(Robert Fillman)

One of the facilities critical to the Army-Navy game operation was **Stadium Tower** (MP 3.9 on the Delaware Extension), so named because of its close proximity to Municipal Stadium (later renamed in memory of John F. Kennedy, the last president to attend the classic in 1962, the year before he was assassinated). Stadium Tower, a two-story concrete block structure with brick trim, controlled the movements from the Delaware Extension in and out of Greenwich Yard. This December 2, 1972 view also shows the steelwork at left for construction of I-95 that parallels the riverfront. *(William Rosenberg)*

This westward view shows the other side of the tower and the yard entrance in a quieter time as Penn Central E44 #4456 backs past to its waiting train on February 22, 1970. In the background is the Broad Street overpass.
(John P. Stroup)

A vast array of equipment was assembled to make up the special trains for the Army-Navy Game operation. Each train was assigned to a particular track in the yard, which was cleared and cleaned up for the occasion. Rail service to the game was inaugurated in 1936 using predominantly GG1's and heavyweight cars, but steam power (mostly K4's) was also used, lasting until 1954. The use of MU equipment, such as the Silverliner II's shown here in November 1969, was begun in the mid-60s. The B&O participated as well, primarily for Navy fans as evidenced here in the background. *(Richard H. Young, Morning Sun Books Collection)*

At the high point of Army-Navy Game operations in 1947, PRR utilized over 300 coaches, 150 Pullmans and nearly 40 dining and lounge cars to accommodate some 28,000 fans to and from the game. A group of enthusiastic Navy fans made their sentiments known while they enjoyed the amenities on board the parlor-drawing room-lounge observation *Queen Mary* (purchased from the Wabash in 1950 and retired from regular service in 1959). PRR ensured that the entire 1967 operation was given the highest priority to provide first-class service.
(Harold A. Smith Collection)

As extensive as it was, the Army-Navy game trains only occupied a portion of vast **Greenwich Point Yard**. This view of MU equipment lined up awaiting the fans' return on November 29, 1969 provides a look at part of the western end of the expansive facility. Strings of hopper cars, the primary use of the yard, are visible in the background. Officially known as the South Philadelphia Terminal Yard at Greenwich Point, it represented a new yard facility south of the old one, constructed beginning in 1928.

This included two receiving yards, a classification and a departure yard. New export coal and import ore piers were also constructed at this time. The yards were reconfigured and enlarged in 1942 and 1944 to handle substantially increased wartime traffic, both for export and to serve the array of military installations in Philadelphia. The total yard capacity was increased from 2,000 to 4,500 cars in 1942, to almost 5,000 cars in 1944 and subsequently to over 6,200 cars.
(Allan H. Roberts)

In December 1972, Penn Central and Amtrak equipment had arrived in the yard for the game. Note the concrete superstructure for I-95 had been completed. The game has also been completed, and the fans are filing past Stadium Tower in an orderly manner to their waiting trains to return home. *(William Rosenberg)*

The export of grain was an early consideration in the layout of rail-water facilities in South Philadelphia. In 1874 PRR constructed the Girard Point Branch extending from the bend in the Delaware Extension southward to Girard Point located between 26th and 29th Street at the outlet of the Schuylkill River. A new terminal was constructed jointly with the International Navigation Company consisting of a large timber grain elevator and storage warehouse. On April 1, 1881 PRR formed the Girard Point Storage Company to take over the operations of the International Navigation Company, but later in the month the elevator burned to the ground. A new one was constructed along with a second elevator to handle the increasing grain tonnage.

In 1912 PRR constructed a massive new one million bushel concrete elevator, its **Girard Point Elevator,** to replace the two old ones at a cost of $760,000. This facility included an elevated steel conveyer system located on the pier that connected to the storage elevator by four conveyor belts, each capable of delivering 15,000 bushels per hour to ships on both sides of the pier. The entire complex had a storage capacity of 2,225,000 bushels in 177 reinforced concrete tanks plus 143 interstice tanks. When the north-south 25th Street Viaduct portion of the Delaware Extension was elevated during the 1920s, the Girard Point complex was served from Penrose Yard alongside the viaduct. On the June 26, 1949 Delaware Extension excursion, photographer Bill Echternacht had the foresight to record this PRR facility. *(Both- William Echternacht)*

PRR completed this export **Coal Pier** on the Delaware Riverfront in 1929, shown here as it appeared 20 years later on that same June 26, 1949 tour. The pier had two rotary dumpers capable of handling nearly 100,000 tons daily. Strings of hoppers were pushed on the two elevated tracks to the dumpers, where individual cars were turned over and unloaded into ships waiting alongside both sides of the pier. The empty cars then rolled down the incline on the river side to the ramps just visible at the end of the pier, and then returned on the two ground-level tracks shown here. The second view provides an indication of the massiveness of the rotary machines compared with the individual on the access stairway. They were 120-ton McMyler units with a maximum capacity of 800 cars per day.

This odd-looking creature was one of two "Barneys" used to push loaded cars up is the inclines. They rolled on their own rails and were operated by the heavy cable connected to a winch at the top of the inclines.
(All- William Echternacht)

A **Warming Shed** was erected to thaw out frozen coal in the hoppers during the winter months. It had a working capacity of sixty 50-ton hoppers or forty-eight 70-ton cars. Note the interesting split frog in the foreground, and in the background at left the nearby ore pier in this March 1959 view.
(Will Coxey, West Jersey Chapter NRHS Collection)

Although an export ore handling facility was part of the 1928-29 yard complex, PRR made a strategic decision to construct a new import **Ore Pier** just north of the coal facility in 1952-54 to unload South American iron ore. Interestingly, the pier itself was built using rubble fill from the then recently-demolished Broad Street Station.

When the $10 million facility was opened, it was equipped with two massive unloading machines that handled over one million tons in the first year. A third machine was added in the following year and a fourth in 1956, expanding total capacity to over 1.5 million tons per year. This superb view made on August 19, 1959 shows all four machines, two having unloaded the ore ship *Ore-Meteor* tied up alongside and the other two poised to attack a newly-arrived ship on the south side of the pier at right. *(G.M. Leilich)*

The ore is unloaded from the ships and then moved by the **Conveyor System** at right either to storage piles or strings of hoppers in the yard. In late 1964, the PRR and U.S. Steel ran their first solid train of foam-insulated ore jennies between this pier and Pittsburgh. The coal dumper is visible under the conveyor superstructure at right in this July 1969 shot. *(Allan H. Roberts)*

At the other end of the main conveyor is this **Distribution Tower** that can be used either to load yard transfer trucks for local transport or the conveyor extension at left to the storage piles or hoppers in the yard. This view of the dusty and noisy operation was made on August 19, 1959. *(G. M. Leilich)*

A view of all four unloaders clustered together on December 1, 1962 provides a transition to a lesser-known carfloat **Transfer Facility** in the distance at left, located on the northern edge of the basin serving the coal and ore piers. *(Emery Gulash, Morning Sun Books Collection)*

The tour group gets an opportunity to view the Transfer Facility close-up, swarming onto the float bridges on June 26, 1949. The Delaware River is subject to tidal variation, necessitating the use of suspended float bridges.

This facility was built during World War II to expedite shipment of heavy equipment overseas. Later it was used as a supplementary way to transfer freight cars to and from the carfloats shown here.

(William Echternacht)

We now move north of Greenwich Point along **Delaware Avenue**. Development of the Delaware River port facilities began in earnest during the period 1871-74. In 1871 the city widened Delaware Avenue, allowing PRR to extend the Delaware Extension north of Greenwich to serve warehouses and piers along the riverfront. In 1874 the line was further extended as far as Dock Street, where a large new freight house was opened. This facility was expanded in 1881 because of growing business. In 1883 PRR built the Swanson Street Branch running north from Greenwich and rejoining the Delaware Extension near Washington Avenue, where the Federal Street Freight Station and an entire complex of yards were built in the ensuing decades into the 20th Century to serve the piers and multiple industries extending northward along the riverfront.

This view shows BS6a switcher #9036 moving a string of cars along Delaware Avenue in May 1962, typifying the street running in this section of Philadelphia. *(Matthew J. Herson, Jr.)*

AS6 #9443 drills cars near the intersection of Oregon and Swanson Streets on February 11, 1967. Note the locomotive has been renumbered in an unusual font in preparation for the Penn Central merger. PRR facilities dominated the area, including an expansive freight terminal and produce yard built in 1925-26, and a large (two million cu-ft) brick cold storage warehouse added in 1928. *(William M. Tilden)*

ARS10s #9915, one of only a handful of steam generator-equipped Alco RS1's owned by PRR, has encountered a bit of a problem. The ice and snow along Delaware Avenue below Snyder Avenue have played havoc with this N&W boxcar in February 1967. *(William M. Tilden)*

Moving farther northward along the riverfront, we come to the **Delaware Avenue Branch.** This line was built in 1882 as the River Front Railroad running north from a connection with the Delaware Extension at Dock Street to the Trenton Avenue Extension south of Frankford Junction, completing a little-known freight loop of the city. This line was formally merged into PRR in 1903. Here BS7 #7900 moves along the branch on Delaware Avenue near Arch Street on February 11, 1967 in the shadow of the Ben Franklin Bridge to New Jersey. *(William M. Tilden)*

Before we move across the Delaware River to New Jersey, we turn to a PRR port facility of a different kind. Ferry service between Philadelphia and Camden was inaugurated by the Camden & Philadelphia Steam Boat Ferry Company in 1838, which was taken over by the Camden & Amboy Railroad later that same year. In 1871 PRR in turn took over the C&P operation by leasing the United New Jersey RRs, which included the C&A and its C&P holdings, including the ferry terminals at the foot of Market Street in Philadelphia and at Federal Street in Camden. In 1899 PRR merged the C&P and the competing West Jersey Ferry Company into the Philadelphia & Camden Ferry Company.

The copper-sheathed **Market Street Ferry Terminal** shown here in March 1952 at the end of service, weathered and without its clocks, was a replacement for an earlier frame structure. In its heyday it was a busy place, served by the Philadelphia Traction Company elevated line that ran along Delaware Avenue past both the PRR terminal at Market Street and the Reading terminals at Chestnut Street. The Ben Franklin Bridge looms in the background, a structure that ultimately led to the demise of all Philadelphia-Camden ferry operations.

To ease the congestion on the ferries, an astounding 38 million passengers in 1925, the Delaware River Bridge (as it was initially known) was opened between Philadelphia and Camden in 1926. Immediately there was a precipitous loss of ferry traffic. To reduce losses, PRR sold off several boats and initially attempted to compete with the bridge by offering reduced fares for heavy trucks. Ferry traffic increased during World War II because of gasoline rationing, but traffic and revenues dropped again after the war ended. PRR increased fares, sold off additional boats and reduced hours of operation, but the ferry finally succumbed to the bridge, with the last run on the evening of March 31, 1952. Two views that same month from the street and water sides record the doomed structure.

(Both- Robert Fillman)

The **Federal Street Terminal** in Camden looks a bit more prosperous in this undated view from the river, although it only hints at the activity seen by this facility in its heyday. The boats are most likely the *Bridgeton*, *Haddonfield* and *Millville*, which served until the end of service in 1952. *(Emil Albrecht, David Cope Collection)*

This expansive facility was opened in 1901 and served for many years as a transportation center, connecting the ferries with a network of railroad, trolley and later bus operations that fanned out in all directions. The front façade of the ferry terminal, facing a large landscaped plaza, is shown here in a circa 1907 postcard view. A trolley stands in front of the wing at left, which was the rail terminal under a large covered trainshed which was later removed, that served PRR and later PRSL trains to southern New Jersey.
(Morning Sun Books Collection)

BORDENTOWN BRANCH / BORDENTOWN SECONDARY

Interlocking	Interlocking Station	Block Station	BORDENTOWN BRANCH BORDENTOWN SECONDARY	*Distance from
			CAMDEN	
			BROADWAY	0.6
X	X	X	CENTER	1.0
X	X	X-O	COOPER	1.5
			PAVONIA	2.5
X	X	X-O	HATCH R–Jersey	
			JERSEY	4.8
			DELAIR	5.0
X		X	MINSON R–Jersey	5.7
			ARCH STREET (Palmyra)	7.1
			PALMYRA	7.7
			RIVERTON	8.3
			CAMBRIDGE	11.0
			RIVERSIDE	11.7
			DELANCO MOVABLE BRIDGE	12.3
			DELANCO	12.4
			PERKINS	13.7
			WALL ROPE WORKS	14.2
			BEVERLY	14.6
			EDGEWATER PARK	15.5
			BURLINGTON	17.4
		B	MJ	18.3
			EAST BURLINGTON	18.4
			STEVENS	19.8
			FLORENCE	22.4
			ROEBLING	23.2
			KINKORA	24.1
			FIELDSBORO	26.0
			DIVISION POST (N. Y.–Phila. Divs.)	26.7
	X		BO R–Fair	26.7
			BORDENTOWN	27.0
			LALOR STREET (Trenton)	31.7
			HAMILTON AVE. (Trenton)	32.7
			TRENTON	33.1
X	X	X-O	FAIR	33.4

HISTORICAL BACKGROUND

Construction of the pioneering Camden & Amboy Railroad began in 1830 at Bordentown and progressed in a northeasterly direction parallel to the Bordentown Turnpike. Bordentown was selected as the starting point because it offered steamboat connections via the Delaware River to Camden and Philadelphia. The C&A completed its track to South Amboy in December 1832, and on January 24, 1833 the first horse-drawn freight operated over the line. With improvements to the roadbed, the road's first locomotive, the *John Bull*, made its maiden round trip between Bordentown and South Amboy in September of that year. The track from Bordentown south along the river to Camden was completed in 1834. Unlike the easy terrain to the north, building the right-of-way south of Bordentown required considerable fill through marshlands and several bridges over the streams draining into the river. Bordentown became the location of the company's headquarters and repair shops as well as the steamboat terminal. The C&A went on to enjoy a monopoly of rail traffic between Philadelphia and the New York City area. However, during the ensuing decades several railroads were constructed on the west side of the Delaware linking these two cities. Once the Connecting Railway was completed in 1867 joining the Philadelphia & Trenton and PRR in Philadelphia, PRR went on to lease the United New Jersey Railroads in 1871 and the C&A routing was relegated to secondary status.

The division assignment of the C&A, and particularly the trackage between Bordentown and Camden, changed over the years, however for purposes of this volume, the Bordentown Secondary Track extends south from Bordentown to Delair and the Bordentown Branch from Delair to Camden.

Burlington (MP 17.4 from Camden) was first organized by Quakers in 1693 and served as the capital of the early province of West Jersey. It was incorporated by royal charter as a city in 1733. After the Revolution it was incorporated by the State of New Jersey in 1784, and enlarged and reincorporated in 1851. The passenger station was originally a frame structure located on the eastward side of the single-track right-of-way in the center of town. By the time of these views made on March 27, 1954 it had been replaced by a compact modern brick building on the south side of town. This structure was opened on October 10, 1949, representing a new standard design. In the first view we find westbound Train #1077 the NELLIE BLY pausing at the station. The second view provides a clear look at the trim single-story brick structure. *(Both- John Dziobko, Jr.)*

June 1963 finds Trenton-Camden Train #2561, a rail motorcar pulling one coach, pausing in Burlington one week before discontinuation of passenger service. The final passenger run between Trenton and Camden occurred on June 28, 1963 using #4666. The event also signaled the final use of rail motorcars on the PRR system. *(Al Holtz)*

Bridge 12.3 or the Delanco Movable Bridge crosses Rancocas Creek, one of the streams draining into the Delaware that the C&A had to span. The bridge consists of a deck plate girder swing span plus timber trestle approaches with concrete abutments. Here Penn Central EF36 #6168 and #6202 move the colorful Strates Shows circus train across the bridge on July 23, 1968. Such a special train was very unusual and worth chasing. *(William M. Tilden)*

Riverside (MP 11.7) was incorporated as a township in 1895 from a portion of Delran Township to the east. The station was located across the tracks from the Philadelphia Watch Case Company building, which once housed the largest watch case manufacturing operation in the country. The distinctive clock tower is now a historic landmark. The station was a single-story frame structure with a brick dado and stucco siding, shown here in an eastward view on April 20, 1974. *(Al Holtz)*

Next we come to **Palmyra** (MP 7.7), which was originally incorporated as a township in 1894 from portions of Cinnaminson Township and Riverton Borough, and reincorporated as a borough in 1923. Here we get a look at this classic gem of a late 19th Century frame freight shed (Type W-12) as it appeared on April 20, 1974, with board-and-batten siding, carved roof brackets and Italianate corbels on the ends. *(Al Holtz)*

The trim station serving **Delair** (MP 5.0) marks the beginning of the Bordentown Branch. The compact single-story frame structure is a variation on Type W-3. This November 9, 1957 view also reveals a variation of a Type W-92 Watch Box in the background. *(John Dziobko, Jr.)*

Pavonia Yard (MP 2.5) was the primary yard facility for Camden. It was laid out in a southwest-northeast direction at the southern end of the Bordentown Branch. Pavonia served that line, the Pemberton Branch, smaller yards and industrial sidings within Camden proper as well as the PRSL lines to South Jersey. Operations in and out of the yard were controlled by Cooper Tower, located at its western end.

These two views depict freights preparing to leave the yard. The first shows renumbered ARS18 #7638 and ARS18a #6873 in charge of westbound freight PT85 on April 29, 1967 outbound on a Pavonia Yard running track. The two closest tracks are designated Cramer 1 and Cramer 2 that were electrified for receiving Motor-powered freights. BS10 units #7991 and #7943, which were maintained by Pavonia Enginehouse, are being deadheaded. The 27th Street overpass spans the yard in the background. The second view made on February 27, 1966 shows two more Alcos, this time AS16m #8603 and AS18am #8676 in charge of Morrisville to Pavonia freight A31 arriving in Pavonia on the westbound main track of the Bordentown Branch. *(Both- William M. Tilden)*

PRR opened this corrugated metal **Pavonia Yard Enginehouse** in 1965 to replace the aged facilities at Camden Terminal which was abandoned to make way for the PATCO transit line. All terminal activity was shifted to Pavonia. This February 1966 view gives us a look at a diverse mixture of predominantly Baldwin power from both PRR and PRSL, both of which used the yard. There are a couple of PRSL RDC's lurking behind the diesels as well. The landmark Camden city hall and courthouse dominate the skyline in the background. *(William M. Tilden)*

Center Tower (MP 1.0) was located at the critical junction of the Bordentown Branch and PRSL trackage to South Jersey Shore points. The substantial two-story brick structure was a typical PRR post-World War I tower design. It was abandoned with Camden Terminal in 1966, and sits a bit worse for wear on March 15, 1968. *(Allan H. Roberts)*

Camden (MP 0.0), the county seat of Camden County and the southern terminus of the Camden & Amboy Railroad, was originally incorporated as a city in 1828. The arrival of the railroad in 1834 brought significant growth in terms of both population and commerce. Long in the shadow of Philadelphia across the river, it gradually evolved into a manufacturing city in its own right, becoming the home of RCA Victor, New York Shipbuilding, Campbell Soup and Esterbrook Pen in addition to many other smaller diverse industries.

Camden also grew in importance as a rail terminal and engine service facility as Bordentown's role diminished considerably. PRR constructed this 20-stall frame roundhouse with corrugated sheathing in 1900 as part of the engine terminal, and built an expanded ferry terminal with attached trainshed in the following year. Veteran B6sb #4035 strikes a classic pose on the turntable on March 2, 1957 in its last year of operation. Diesels also used this facility until the new enginehouse was built in Pavonia Yard. *(Ralph Phillips Collection)*

The riverfront **Camden Terminal Enginehouse** facilities included this massive concrete coaling wharf and sand facility. The adjacent wooden water tank was most likely a 24,000-gallon Type TW-25 with Type TFS-25 steel frame supports and a frost box.

These facilities were still in service when this photo was taken in January 1956. Note the coal hopper positioned at the conveyor at right. In the background are two more Camden landmarks – the RCA Building at left and the Campbell Soup plant at right. *(Al Holtz)*

By March 1968 steam was long gone and so is the water tank, although the standpipe remains in place. The coal wharf still stands, however, a silent sentinel to its long years of service. The rains have washed away much of the accumulated soot from the pall of smoke that hung over the Camden Yards for decades.

Large industrial structures such as this one make compelling photographic subjects, as evidenced by this close-up of the standpipe dwarfed by the massive wharf with its chute mechanism. By the time this study was made the yard tracks had been torn up as well, leaving a sea of ties and other industrial debris on the riverfront.

(All- Allan H. Roberts)

DELAWARE RIVER RAILROAD & BRIDGE COMPANY

Interlocking	Interlocking Station	Block Station	DELAWARE RIVER RAILROAD & BRIDGE COMPANY
			D. R. R. R. & B. CO. BRANCH (Including Main Line, Philadelphia Division, to Vernon)
X	X	X-O	SHORE..
			FRANKFORD JUNCTION............
X	X	X-O	JERSEY... 1
X			DIVIDE—R-Jersey................... 1
			JORDAN... 1
			RACE.. 1
			DIVISION POST (Phila. Div.) 969 feet North of Vernon Interlocking Station...........
X	B	B	VERNON (P.R.S.L.).................... 1

HISTORICAL BACKGROUND

The short Delaware River Railroad & Bridge Company line was constructed by PRR in conjunction with the Delair Bridge and opened in April 1896 at a cost of $145 million. It established for the first time a rail connection between the Philadelphia-New York main (at Frankford Junction) and the parallel Camden & Amboy line in New Jersey, thus providing access to Camden and PRR's expanding array of branches to New Jersey shore points. Its electrification between Frankford Junction and Pavonia was removed by PRR in the fall of 1966 only to be restored by Penn Central in May 1973.

The original **Delair Bridge** (Bridge 2.07) over the Delaware River was made up of three double-track through truss spans plus a swing drawbridge supported on stone piers, for a total length of 1932'. The approaches were deck truss viaducts on either side: the long west approach (Bridge 1.88) began over Frankford Junction Yard and consisted of 52 plate girder spans totaling 2131'; the east approach (#2.28) was considerably shorter. In 1960 PRR replaced the truss just west of the swing drawbridge with a 543' vertical lift span to allow for greater clearance for the ever larger ships on the river. The end of the first truss was foreshortened to make room for erection of two massive lift towers on new concrete piers. Following typical PRR procedure, the lift span was floated into position to minimize delays and became the longest and heaviest lift bridge in the world. The mechanism was then removed from the swing span and its position secured.

Here's our circus train again, this time in an interesting move as Penn Central EF36 #6168 and #6202 back the Strates Shows special train eastward across the bridge on June 23, 1968. Note the round stone pier originally supporting the swing span and the newer concrete piers for the lift towers. *(William M. Tilden)*

Coming off the east end of the bridge, trains had two options at appropriately-named Jersey Interlocking. A diverting southward route toward Camden onto the Bordentown Branch lead to Pavonia Yard, as this freight is doing on February 19, 1966. The straight route continued east to shore points. **Jersey Tower** (MP 11.0 from Suburban Station) is a two-story brick structure that controlled this junction, which was used by PRR freights and PRSL passenger trains. It was built in the summer of 1937, replacing four smaller wood frame structures. In addition to controlling the junction, the tower also protected the bridge openings – all home signals were set to "stop" and the smash boards were lowered. The tower also remotely controlled Divide Interlocking, located just east of Jersey, which was at the Bordentown Branch connection used by the New York-Atlantic City trains, and Mission and Hatch Interlockings, located north and south, respectively, of Jersey on the Bordentown Branch.
(William M. Tilden)

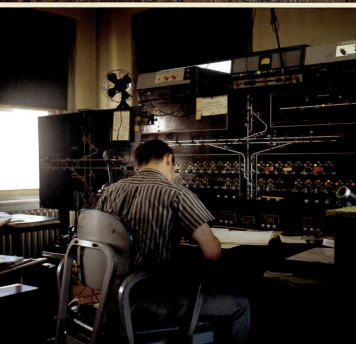

Penn Central tower operator Marty Hahn keeps up with his paperwork between trains in Jersey Tower on August 21, 1969. The ancient fan strikes a contrast with the much newer radio communications equipment on top of the panel, which is oriented with the bridge to the left.
(John P. Stroup)

Continuing southward on the short Bridge Branch is **Jordan** block station (MP 12.9). The primary purpose of this small frame watch box (similar to Type W-91) was to shelter block operators on duty for troop train movements to Fort Dix, the large U.S. Army base accessed by a connection to the Pemberton Branch, which crossed over on a bridge just south of this point. In this view eastbound Philadelphia-Atlantic City PRSL Train #1001 is headed by Baldwin AS16 #6015 on May 23, 1965. The short consist reflects declining patronage for such service at this time. *(William M. Tilden)*

PEMBERTON BRANCH / BIRMINGHAM SECONDARY

HISTORICAL BACKGROUND

After completion of the pioneering Camden & Amboy Railroad linking those two New Jersey towns in 1834, interest turned toward accessing the interior of Burlington County. Accordingly, the Burlington & Mount Holly Railroad & Transportation Company was incorporated in 1848 to connect Burlington on the C&A with Mount Holly, the county seat of Burlington County. The line was extended eastward from Mount Holly to Pemberton in 1863 and the name of the road changed to the Burlington County Railroad Company. A short branch was built southward from Evansville to Vincentown in the following year.

In the meantime, the Camden, Moorestown, Hainesport & Mount Holly Horse Car Railroad was incorporated in 1859 to construct a line from Camden to connect with the BCRR at Mount Holly. However, before this line was finished the company was consolidated with the BCRR in 1866 to become the Camden & Burlington County Railroad Company, which completed the 16.25-mile road in the following year. A six-mile line to Medford was built in 1869 by the Mount Holly, Lumberton & Medford Railroad Company. PRR leased all of these lines in 1871 with the UNJRR.

Without burdening the reader with even more early history, in 1915 a complex series of railroad line consolidations took place, extending the PRR system eastward to multiple New Jersey shore points via the C&BC and the Pennsylvania & Atlantic Railroad Company. This brief examination of rail facilities will confine itself to the lines that became the PRR Pemberton Branch to that community, and the Birmingham Secondary extending east from Birmingham to Toms River. The designated railroad direction from Camden to Toms River varied over time, but during this period it was southward.

Interlocking	Interlocking Station	Block Station	Block-Limit Station	PEMBERTON BRANCH / BIRMINGHAM SECONDARY
				PEMBERTON BRANCH DIX RUNNING TRACK
X	X	X-O		COOPER
		X		STATE STREET......R-Cooper
				PAVONIA
				WEST MERCHANTVILLE
				MERCHANTVILLE
				PENNSAUKEN
				MAPLE SHADE
				LENOLA
				WEST MOORESTOWN
				MOORESTOWN
				STANWICK AVE.
				HARTFORD
				MASONVILLE
				HAINESPORT
		B		MOUNT HOLLY C-Cooper
				SMITHVILLE
				EWANSVILLE
		B		BIRMINGHAM C-Cooper
		X		PEMBERTON C-Cooper
				PEMBERTON
				SHREVE
				LEWIS	Dix Running Track
				CAMP (U. T. Co.)

After the closing of the Camden Terminal passenger facility with the end of Philadelphia-Camden ferry service in 1952, **Broadway Station** (MP 0.6) was rebuilt and enlarged to become the primary terminal in New Jersey for Pemberton Branch and other southern New Jersey point trains. Here, Camden to Pemberton local Train #983 eases into the station still behind steam in the form of K4s #3872. The locomotive looks in reasonable condition and has a clean stack, but its days are numbered – the date is August 1957, and the end of steam is near. In fact the final steam-powered passenger train on the entire PRR system was Pemberton to Camden local Train #982 on November 12, 1957, pulled by K4s #5351. *(Al Holtz)*

By 1965 the patronage and number of trains had declined further and the platform canopies (and overall maintenance, by the looks of things) were cut back. The reduced facility provides a clear look at the station configuration, two concrete platforms with steel canopies extending from the twin waiting rooms. In a rather forlorn scene, Train #990 from Moorestown waits on Track #3 on the day before Christmas. The safety stripes and headlights were added on the car ends to improve visibility when the train backed during deadhead moves.

(William M. Tilden)

Pemberton Branch freights originated in **Pavonia Yard** (MP 2.5), as evidenced here as PRR BS10as #5592 heads local CB20 over freshly-ballasted track on September 23, 1966 shortly after the yard was rebuilt and enlarged. The yard is located in east Camden at the junction of the Bordentown and Pemberton branches. Cooper Tower controlled the south end of the yard as well as the Pemberton Branch connection.

Photographer Tilden captured PRR Moorestown to Camden deadhead train Train #990 headed by rare PRR BS12as #8975 as it crossed over the South Branch of Pennsauken Creek on April 8, 1966. The attractive stone arch **Bridge 6.62** located between Pennsauken and Maple Shade was constructed in 1888. A companion twin arch concrete structure (#8.01), built in 1913 between Maple Shade and Lenola, spans the North Branch. While both of these structures are wide enough for double track, the entire line is single track with passing sidings. Between 1917 and 1932, five miles between Mount Holly and Birmingham had been double-tracked *(Both- William M. Tilden)*

Enough of the arch windows and Victorian carving on the roof brackets of the single-story frame **Moorestown** station (MP 10.4) can be made out to justify including this image in a facilities volume. But April 25, 1969 was a sad day. This photo records the final day of passenger service on the Pemberton Branch, as Train #990, consisting of BS12am #8084 and coach #1046, make their way for the last time from Moorestown to Camden.

The area now known as Moorestown was settled by Quakers beginning around 1680 in an area then known as Rodmantown (western portion) and Chestertown (eastern portion) – the area gradually came to be known as Moorestown in the mid-1850s, after Moore's Tavern. The only way to travel between Camden and Moorestown was by stagecoach until the C&BC was built in 1867. The town was finally incorporated in 1922. *(John P. Stroup)*

Two years earlier, the morning Pemberton-Camden Train #988 approaches a position light signal at Moorestown on April 3, 1967. The Pemberton Branch was operated under Manual Block System rules 305-315 and 317-342.
(William M. Tilden)

Here's another stretch for a facilities volume, but concrete **Bridge 13.59** over Parkers Creek supports the railroad right-of-way as Train #988 with a single coach heads toward Camden south of Hartford on April 26, 1967.
(William M. Tilden)

We now move to **Mount Holly** (MP 18.7) and a real gem of a station, typical of early railroad station construction and similar to the one at Moorestown. The one-story frame structure is a study in mid-19th Century architecture, with its board-and-batten siding, carved roof bracket trim and Italianate end corbels. It was used for passenger service and still displays a classic enameled steel Railway Express Agency sign in this June 24, 1957 view.

Mount Holly was formed in 1688 as Northampton, which subsequently became one of New Jersey's initial 104 towns incorporated in 1798. Portions of the town were used to form several other townships and boroughs over the ensuing decades, and the town was renamed Mount Holly in 1931. Several early mills were established on Rancocas Creek in the early 1700s, and the New Jersey authorized the relocation of the Burlington County seat from Burlington City to Mount Holly in 1793, thus spurring development of the area as a destination for rail lines to the interior of the county. The Burlington & Mount Holly arrived in 1849, and 20 years later the C&BC constructed the station in town. *(John Dziobko, Jr.)*

This view shows the other end of the station as it appeared circa 1957. Beyond the motor railcar is a crossing shanty (PRR Watch Box Type W-91) and behind it the frame freight station. At one time a five-stall roundhouse and small yard were located behind the freight house.

The junction with the Medford Branch was located a little over a quarter mile beyond the freight house which was destroyed by fire, although a concrete loading platform and ramp were subsequently built on the site. *(W. Broschart, Harold A. Smith Collection)*

This unusual shelter served the community of **Evansville** (MP 22.0). Although there were several small frame shelters on the branch, this was the only one on the line of poured reinforced concrete construction. The structure has suffered many indignities as this March 1983 view attests, but its molded-on keystone endures. Evansville was once the site of CG Block Station, a one-story 8x9' frame building controlling two signals. *(Rich Taylor)*

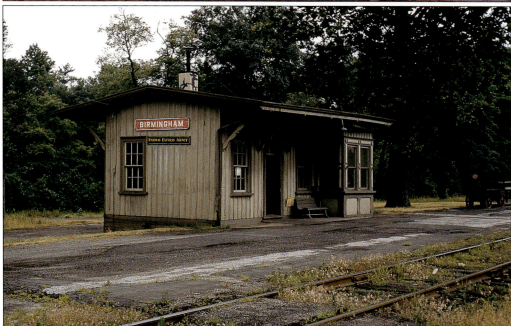

This trim frame station served **Birmingham** (MP 22.4), located at the junction of the C&BC and the Pennsylvania & Atlantic line to Bay Head Junction. It is a variation of Type W-1, with carved roof brackets and detailed moldings on the offset operator's bay. The station served as a block station, which also controlled the junction, until it was abolished circa 1964. A large volume of raw milk was shipped in cans from the station until trucks took over the task. The attractive structure was still functional as a passenger station on June 24, 1957, complete with Railway Express sign and baggage wagon. *(John Dziobko, Jr.)*

Heading up the line toward Fort Dix, we come to the station at **Pemberton** (MP 22.4 – formerly North Pemberton), which was constructed in the mid-1890s. It is a substantial brick structure with wide dormers similar to Type B-2. This view gives us another look at a last scheduled passenger train on April 25, 1969, as Train #988 makes its final journey to Camden behind BS12am #8084. Pemberton was incorporated in 1826 within New Hanover and Northampton Townships, and became an independent borough around 1894. *(William M. Tilden)*

Toms River (MP 50.9) was located at the end of the Birmingham Secondary. These two views show the interesting two-story frame passenger station, likely including the agent's quarters, a variation of Type 2W-6 and the adjacent frame freight house. A rail motorcar and RPO-baggage trailer grace the scene in April 1951. The last passenger run between Birmingham and Toms River occurred a year later on June 21, 1952. Interestingly, the station was eventually moved and as this is written in 2008, serves nearby as a private residence.

Looking across the track we find a wooden water tank. Likely a 10,000-gallon type TW-10 and its trackside standpipe, in addition to a perfect example of a Type W-91 watch box, all in reasonably good shape. On the ground next to the watch box is what appears to be an earlier tank roof structure.

Toms River, whose name is attributed to various sources, was the site of a salt works that supplied colonial militias until it was destroyed by British and Loyalist troops in 1782. It became a center for shipbuilding, whaling and fishing, and later iron and lumber production in the 19th Century. Toms River was designated the county seat of the newly-created Ocean County in 1850. *(All- John Dziobko, Jr.)*

MAIN LINE

ZOO TOWER TO PARKESBURG

Interlocking	Interlocking Station	Block Station	ZOO TOWER TO PARKESBURG	Distance from Jersey City
X	X	X-O	ZOO (44th St.)	3.2
			52nd STREET	3.9
X			VALLEY—R-Overbrook	4.0
X	X	X-O	OVERBROOK	5.4
			OVERBROOK	5.4
			MERION	6.0
			NARBERTH	6.8
			WYNNEWOOD	7.4
			ARDMORE	8.5
			HAVERFORD	9.1
			BRYN MAWR	10.1
X	B	B	BRYN MAWR	10.1
			ROSEMONT	10.9
			VILLANOVA	12.0
			RADNOR	13.0
			ST. DAVIDS	13.7
			WAYNE	14.5
			STRAFFORD	15.4
			DEVON	16.4
			BERWYN	17.5
			DAYLESFORD	18.6
			PAOLI	19.8
X	X	X	PAOLI	19.9
			MALVERN	21.8
			FRAZER	23.7
X			GLEN—R-Thorn	25.3
			WHITFORD	28.2
X			DOWNS—R-Thorn	32.1
			DOWNINGTOWN	32.3
X	X	X	THORN	35.0
			THORNDALE	35.0
X			CALN—R-Thorn	36.6
			COATESVILLE	38.4
			POMEROY	41.9
X	X	X-O	PARK	43.9
			PARKESBURG	44.2
			DIVISION POST (Harrisburg Division)	45.0

HISTORICAL BACKGROUND

We now move to the east-west Main Line west of Zoo Tower as far as the Division Post with the Harrisburg Division at Parkesburg. Like much of railroad history in the eastern U.S., it all began with the visionary Col. John Stevens, whom we met in the New York Division volumes. As early as 1823, he obtained the first charter for a rail line to be built from Philadelphia westward to Columbia on the Susquehanna River. However, this line and a subsequent venture both came to naught in the face of vigorous opposition from the near-fanatic canal advocates. In response to these forces in 1825 (the year New York's landmark Erie Canal was completed), the Pennsylvania Legislature established a permanent Canal Commission of its own, which was authorized to survey a route for a canal across the Commonwealth.

Although work on the canal actually began in 1826 westward from a point on the Susquehanna near present-day Middletown, Major John Wilson of the U.S. Topographical Engineers recommended building a railroad rather than a canal across the eastern part of the state because of the undulating terrain. Major Wilson, his son and a young assistant named John Edgar Thomson laid out a route from the hill above the Schuylkill River through the Chester Valley and then to Columbia. The resultant Philadelphia & Columbia Railroad became the eastern leg of the Main Line of Public Works, the planned system of canals and railroads running across the Commonwealth from Philadelphia to Pittsburgh, an entity approved by the Legislature in 1828.

Work on the P&C began in 1829, and after a series of delays was finally completed in 1834. The line began at the terminal built at Broad and Vine Streets in Philadelphia, ran northward parallel to the Schuylkill River, then crossed the river and ascended a 2,805' inclined plane at Belmont to the crest of the valley, where it ran westward and then descended into the Susquehanna Valley by means of another plane for a total of 81 miles. Here the traveler had to transfer to a canal boat at the Susquehanna River for a 173-mile journey on the Pennsylvania Canal to Hollidaysburg, where the boats were lifted over the mountains via the 36-mile Allegheny Portage Railroad, and finally completing the last 104 miles to Pittsburgh by canal.

The State Works continued to be used for some time, although funds for maintenance were problematic and the entire system began to deteriorate. Meanwhile, the advantages of rail roads began to become apparent to even the most fervent canal devotees. Two short lines were built in the period 1834-39 that would eventually provide a westward connection for the P&C, namely, the Harrisburg & Lancaster, which was later extended to Columbia as the Harrisburg & Columbia, and the Cumberland Valley Railroad to the southwest.

But it was not until 1846, when a group of enterprising Philadelphia businessmen organized to form the Pennsylvania Railroad, that a continuous rail line across the Commonwealth would come to fruition. PRR was chartered in April 1846 to build a railroad from Harrisburg to Pittsburgh, overcoming just barely opposition from both canal forces and rival B&O. Thomson was named Chief Engineer, and then, through a combination of engineering genius and sheer determination, pushed construction of the railroad right-of-way though river valleys where possible and carving his way up the side of mountain slopes to finally reach Pittsburgh by an all-rail route in 1855, when the railroad was considered "complete." Demonstrating political savvy and financial acumen during the process, he took over as president in 1852, brushing aside those reluctant to continue to finance construction.

But although PRR had taken over operation of the H&C in 1848, it was still dependent on the operation of the P&C for its eastern connection to Philadelphia. Thomson was convinced that because of the high tolls and delays due both to seasonal closings and poor trackwork, much traffic from the West was being handled over other routes, including the B&O and the Erie. After attempts, thwarted by the canal forces, to gain operating rights on the P&C, PRR was finally successful in 1853, but only for passenger trains. But Thomson wanted complete control. After three years of high-stakes negotiations, he was ultimately successful in taking over the entire State Works for $7.5 million in July 1857.

PRR now had a rail line into Philadelphia that it could call its own. But what PRR had acquired was in poor condition. Although the P&C had replaced both the early Belmont and Columbia planes that carried it into the Schuylkill and Susquehanna Valleys with new alignments in 1840 and 1850 respectively, and some trackwork and bridge repair had been carried out in response to public pressure, the railroad needed complete rebuilding. The track was re-laid with new T-section rail on wider centers with new ties and ballast, bridges were rebuilt and the sharpest curves reduced. In addition new stations were built at many locations on the line.

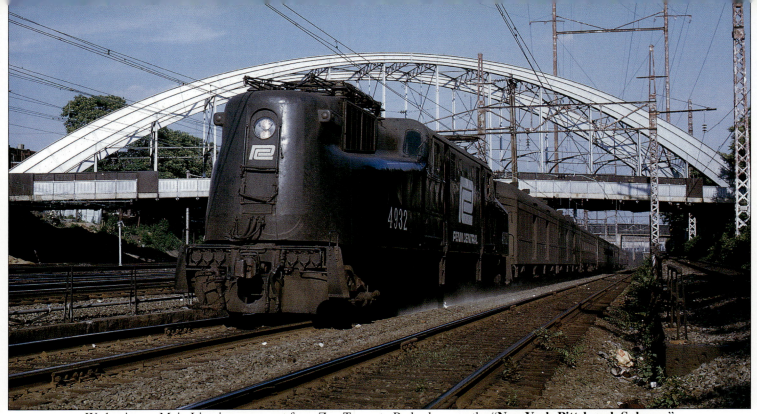

We begin our Main Line journey west from Zoo Tower to Parkesburg on the "**New York-Pittsburgh Subway**," an aptly named leg of Zoo Interlocking. In June 1969, Train #31, the combined Spirit of St. Louis / Cincinnati Limited, kicks up the dust as it accelerates under overhead **Bridge 3.03** (42nd Street). *(William J. Brennan)*

In addition to the large 1876 Centennial Depot at the corner of 32nd and Market Streets, PRR built a temporary station directly in front of the main entrance to the Exposition grounds to handle the large crowds traveling by rail to the site. It also laid out a storage yard along the main west of Mantua Junction, later Zoo, and a turning loop to allow access to the station from either direction. After the Exposition closed the station and most of the loop were removed, but the yards were expanded dramatically over the years to fill the entire 85 acre property that PRR had acquired between Mantua Avenue and 52nd Street. A freight depot originally located near the site of the new station was later moved to the 52nd Street end.

This early 1950s view shows the **52nd Street Yards** looking eastward from the approach to the jumpover bridge connecting to the Schuylkill Branch. The yard consisted of three classification yards, A, B, and C, to the right north of the main and transfers and overflow yards behind. Beyond that in the center of the photo is the coaling wharf marking the 46th Street Engine Terminal placed in service in January 1930. To the left of the coaling tower is the green dome of Memorial Hall, a remnant of the Centennial Exposition.

(Morning Sun Books Collection)

The first engine facility in the 52nd Street yard area was an eight-stall roundhouse of frame construction with corrugated iron sheathing built in 1887-8 near 46th Street. This was replaced with a brick structure in 1902, along with a machine shop, power plant and coal wharf. The roundhouse was enlarged to 16 stalls in 1912 and lengthened in 1918 to accommodate larger locomotives. Additional shop buildings were also added at that time to the growing complex, known as the Park Shops, after the adjacent Fairmount Park, a portion of which occupied the former Exposition grounds.

A new 26-stall brick, concrete and timber-framed roundhouse was constructed in 1930 along the eastern edge of the yard, north of the existing structures, which were then demolished. The $1.5 million complex, which became known as the **46th Street Engine Terminal**, included a roundhouse with a 110' turntable, a massive 600-ton concrete coaling tower, machine and fabrication shops, two 100,000-gallon steel water tanks and a 220' long ash pit. This view looks east at the roundhouse and turntable on June 11, 1966. *(Allan H. Roberts)*

The new engine terminal, part of the comprehensive Philadelphia Improvements program, replaced one of the roundhouses in the West Philadelphia Yard, allowing expansion of the passenger car storage tracks for equipment serving the new 30th Street and Suburban Stations. The 46th Street complex became the center for steam locomotive service in the Philadelphia area, and some electric motors were also serviced here as well. Its usefulness declined after the end of steam, although it continued to serve the diesel fleet into the Penn Central era, as exemplified by this collection of unusual units idling alongside the roundhouse on May 11, 1969. Engine #8062 is a truly rare bird, one of only two ex-NYC Lima-Hamilton LS1200RS roadswitchers repowered by EMD and assigned to Philadelphia. Alco #9916 (center) is a one-of-a-kind ex-PRR ARS10xs, with AS10 #9964, another ex-NYC unit, in the rear. *(William M. Tilden)*

A quiet August 5, 1963 finds more traditional PRR power at rest at 46th Street. *(Ralph Phillips Collection)*

85

We now move westward to **Overbrook Tower** (MP 5.4), the first tower at the eastern end of the near-legendary PRR Main Line. It is located on the south side of the mainline, just east of Overbrook Station, and housed a 19-lever electro-pneumatic machine. Here an inbound morning local pauses at the station on June 4, 1968.
(William M. Tilden)

Here's a look at the west side of the two-story brick structure on October 1, 1981, with its Amtrak signage. The tower was responsible for controlling the complete set of crossovers at this location, the westward end of the 59th Street Receiving Yard and at this time remotely the interlockings on the eastern end of the Schuylkill Branch.
(Harold A. Smith)

Overbrook (MP 5.4) is the oldest surviving PRR station on the Philadelphia Division. The two-story frame central structure with board-and-batten siding, housing the waiting room, ticket office and agent's quarters, was built on the eastbound side of the tracks in 1866. The wood frame shelter sheds (Type W-33) were added to the original structure and the westbound shelter when the station was expanded in 1912. The concrete overpass bridge carries City Line Avenue (originally at grade) over the busy four-track mainline in a November 1966 view.
(Emery Gulash, Morning Sun Books Collection)

The station was given an Amtrak paint scheme in the 1970s. Even when new it was a garish addition and became worse when it faded. At least it provided some protection to the exquisitely carved Victorian trim until a more thorough and accurate restoration was undertaken early in the 21st Century. For better or worse, this view showed the appearance at the westward end of the westbound shelter, complete with graffiti, on October 1, 1981 as a pair of Silverliners approach. *(Harold A. Smith)*

This attractive one-story brick and stucco station (a variant of Type B1, with canopy extensions) was built at **Merion** (MP 6.0) just prior to World War I. It had the dubious distinction of being the last new station built on the Main Line until Paoli was rebuilt over 35 years later. These October 1, 1981 views also provide a look at the freight station of matching construction located on the westbound side. Interestingly, the original main station at Merion was a wood frame structure built in 1864 and located on the westbound side. It was later expanded with platform canopies and an eastbound shelter added. The replacement westbound structure is shown here. *(Both- Harold A. Smith)*

The original station serving **Narberth** (MP 6.8) was a small two-story stone structure built on the westbound side in 1870, the date of several new stations after a major track relocation program following the Civil War. The area was known as Elm at the time and was a convenient destination for city residents escaping the heat during the summer. The station was subsequently renamed Narberth by president George Roberts, one of several given Welsh names to attract the upscale clientele PRR was trying to cultivate. The westbound structure was replaced 100 years later, but the frame eastbound shelter, Type W-35, with curved brackets, shown here in May 1975 dates from circa 1890.

A westbound commuter train pauses at the attractive two-story (one story at track level) brick structure of distinctly modern design built in 1969, making it the newest station on the Main Line. The curve beyond the station marks the beginning of the "Great Fill" between Narberth and Wynnewood.

(Both- Harold A. Smith)

The station built at **Wynnewood** (MP 7.4) was another small stone structure built in 1870, but this one has survived. Platform shelters were added in the late 19th Century and then extended in 1910. Originally known as Libertyville, the community was renamed for Thomas Wynne, who led the first colonial assembly convened by William Penn in 1683. An eastbound Silverliner pauses to pick up passengers on October 1, 1981. The westbound shelter is shown here the same day with Amtrak track equipment working on Tracks #2 and 3. This structure dates from the late 19th Century and is a variant of Type W-35 frame construction. Wynnewood is located at the westward end of the broad sweeping curve and immense fill beginning at Narberth, which was part of a track elevation project to reduce grades and road crossings through the area. *(Both- Harold A. Smith)*

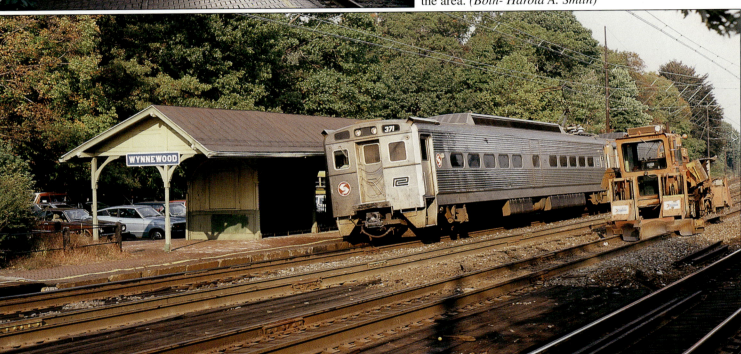

The old stone station survives, with the added role of an Irish bake shop, seen here on August 14, 2001. *(Dr. Art Peterson)*

We are very fortunate in having these winter 1957 views of the stunning two-story stone Victorian station built in 1873 at **Ardmore** (MP 8.5) by the Philadelphia firm of Wilson Brothers, responsible for Broad Street Station, the two largest buildings in the Centennial Exposition and several other Philadelphia landmarks. It can be considered the most ornate station built on the Main Line, a stunning example of Gothic Revival architecture.

It was a U-shaped structure with a large crossed-gable wing on the eastward end and an ornate tower at the westward end, which housed a block station for several years. Like several others, as built the station had broad wooden platforms, which were cut back as the third and fourth tracks were added. The platform shelters were extended in 1906 and again in 1909 to handle growing traffic. Train #23 THE MANHATTAN LIMITED highballs through the station bound for Chicago.

The second view shows the eastbound shelter as an eastbound coal train shoved by BS24m #8727 rumbles through. Sadly the station was demolished later in 1957, the first victim of a new PRR program to sell off stations where possible to cut property taxes.

Ardmore, formerly Athensville, was the point at which the original route of the P&C via the Belmont Plane joined the new alignment completed in 1840.

(Both- Will Coxey, West Jersey Chapter NRHS Collection)

Haverford (MP 9.1) was the home of early woolen mills along with Haverford College, established by Quakers to foster classical education. The westbound station depicted here on July 25, 1988 was still another small stone structure built in 1870. The platform shelters were extended in 1906 and a baggage shed added in 1913. For a time in the 1950's, the Haverford station housed the offices of Manor Real Estate and other non-railroad PRR subsidiaries.

The second view was taken from the eastbound side on August 11, 1983, in front of the two-story brick and concrete station (one-story at track level) built on that side in 1916. This structure housed a post office on the first floor at street level, and the waiting room and ticket office at track level. *(Both- Harold A. Smith)*

Here's a street-level view of the station, which housed an insurance office as well as the post office on August 13, 2001. *(Dr. Art Peterson)*

A patina of road grime coats a pair of workhorse E44's and reminds us of the weariness of Eastern railroading on this September 21, 1974. Plans were a-cookin' down in Washington, D.C. that would further submerge the PRR into mega rail systems. *(Harold A. Smith)*

In 1868 the PRR Board approved a major track realignment project to eliminate the sharp curves between Haverford and West Haverford (later Rosemont). The effort, completed in 1870, resulted in the intermediate station stop being relocated from Whitehall north to **Bryn Mawr** (MP 10.1 – another Welsh name), where a large two-story stone station was built in that year, again by Wilson Brothers. The elegant Gothic Revival structure, second only to the one at Ardmore, served the well-heeled clientele who traveled to the fashionable Bryn Mawr Hotel resort constructed in 1873, the same year that the double track was extended westward to this point.

The first view looking eastward in September 1966 shows the platform of the matching stone freight station on the right, built east of the passenger station and enlarged in 1916-17. GG1 #4889 leads a westbound passenger train past the two-story concrete substation, constructed in 1915 to supply power to this section when the Main Line was electrified.

The passenger station was enlarged and remodeled in 1900, with extended platform canopies and a baggage house added at that time. This structure served until a modest but attractive new single-story brick station was built just to the east in 1963-64. The new station is just visible under the platform canopy as an eastbound local picks up passengers in September 1966. The fencing marks the site of the old station, which had been demolished.

The westbound shelter dates from 1900, with an enclosed shed at the westward end (Type S-36) and an open steel-framed canopy to the east. Old and new MU equipment pass that same September 1966 day.
(All- William Rosenberg)

Bryn Mawr Tower is located just to the west of the station also at MP 10.1. The two-story brick and frame structure was built in 1896. It houses a 25-lever electric machine to control this section of the mainline plus the crossovers that allow MU locals terminating at Bryn Mawr to cross over from Track #4 to Track #1 for the return run to Philadelphia. Westbound Train #341, consisting of a trio of Silverliner II's, passes the tower on June 6, 1968. The catenary poles in this section are the original tubular design installed on the Main Line in 1913-15. *(William M. Tilden)*

Keeping the line open and free of ice and snow sometimes requires large pieces of equipment, but more often involves much smaller, but still vital, items. These switch heaters, shown here being refilled with kerosene after a storm in January 1970 are one example. All power switches must be kept clear of snow and especially ice to operate dependably. *(David Cope)*

Rosemont (MP 10.9) was named after the estate of Joshua Ashbridge, who donated a piece of property for the construction of the station originally known as West Haverford. The location was moved a short distance westward onto the new alignment in 1871. The brick and stucco structure shown here in an eastward view on September 21, 1974 was built in 1891-92, and enlarged in 1906 and again in 1909. The westbound shelter is largely obscured by the quartet of newly-delivered Silverliner IV's, but we can see enough to classify it as Type W-35 with curved brackets. *(Both- Harold A. Smith)*

Villanova (MP 12.0) was another stone station, a two-story structure built in 1872 and extended in 1906. It serves the town and namesake university, some of whose buildings are just visible under the overpass on June 14, 1975. The overpass structure seen here replaced an early PRR tied-arch truss later utilized as a road bridge. *(Dr. Art Peterson)*

The original station at Morgan's Corner, later **Radnor,** (MP 13.0) was a frame structure built on the eastbound side in 1862. It was replaced in 1871 by the two-story brick station shown here in September 1965. The station was extended in 1902 and again in 1906 with the Type W-33 wood frame platform canopies. *(William J. Brennan)*

Photographer Al Holtz was riding back from Norristown on the Philadelphia & Western rapid transit line in 1958 when he decided to get out at Radnor and make the quarter-mile trek over to the PRR station. There he recorded Train #33 the westbound St. Louisian laden with mail and express cars. The P&W crossed under the PRR Main Line three-tenths of a mile east of the station at milepost 12.70. There was no thought of a joint station, however, as both roads were competing for the same traffic when built. Al then continued on to Ardmore Junction where he boarded an Ardmore trolley for the journey back to 69th Street Terminal in Philadelphia. *(Al Holtz)*

Here's a better look at the frame shelter shed on the westbound side (Type W-35 again with curved brackets).

This May 1981 view shows fencing has been added between the eastbound and westbound tracks to prevent passengers from crossing the busy railroad. *(Harold A. Smith)*

An upscale community was laid out at **St. Davids** (MP 13.7), originally known as East Wayne, in the late 1880s to attract wealthy Philadelphians to the area. PRR obliged by constructing an ornate two-story frame structure on the eastbound side in 1890 similar to the one at Rosemont. It was torn down in October 1966 and replaced with simple shelters shown here on May 10, 1975. A power move of E44's and GG1's provides variety from the seemingly endless procession of MU cars prevalent on this line.

The second view on the same day shows the ticket office relocated to a small frame structure on the westbound side as a pair of newly-purchased Silverliner IV's picks up passengers.
(Both- Harold A. Smith)

Wayne (MP 14.5) was another community where the station was heavily influenced by early real estate developers. The first station was a two-story frame structure built in 1873 at what was then known as Cleaver's Landing. It served as a milk stop for the rural area as well as a very early residential development known as Louella. The tract was sold in 1880 and renamed Wayne Estate. The second station was relocated at that time from the Centennial Exposition grounds, however, a new and larger development resulted in construction of a third station (Type 2B-3) designed by Wilson Brothers in 1883. The second station was moved westward to Strafford, enlarged in 1903 making it symmetrical, and a freight house added in 1905. The attractive two-story frame structure is shown here as it appeared on September 14, 1974. The westbound shelter (Type W-35) was built in 1902 and extended like several others in 1906. *(Harold A. Smith)*

And now we come to the jewel of Main Line stations, the ornamental confection serving **Strafford** (MP 15.4). Fortunately we are able to examine all four sides of this delightful structure. Originally built for the 1876 Centennial Exposition, most likely as a catalogue building, it was moved first to Wayne as a flag stop and then circa 1885 to this location, originally called Eagle after an early tavern. The left view shows the eastward side on July 25, 1981 with the sun and contrasting paint scheme highlighting the exquisitely detailed woodwork. The right view shows the track (north) side on the same date. The steel-frame shelter shed (Type S-35) was a later addition. *(Both- Harold A. Smith)*

Moving to the west side, we can see the covered stairway leading to the parking lot on street level in July 1981. The station was renamed Strafford in 1887 after a large estate nearby.
(Harold A. Smith)

Finally we get a look at the south side from the parking lot on January 24, 1976. These last two views serve to portray not only the two-story station, but also the right-of-way elevated on a fill, the result of PRR's efforts to smooth out gradients and eliminate grade crossings. *(Al Holtz)*

Devon (MP 16.4) is the location of the world-renowned Devon Horse Show, a Main Line tradition established on a site across Lancaster Avenue from the station in the 1890s. The two-story brick and stucco structure was built in 1883 on the eastbound side, the westbound shelter (Type W-35) was added in 1902 and a baggage house in 1905. This view looks eastward in May 1970 as a trio of westbound Silverliners reach the shelter. *(Will Coxey, West Jersey Chapter NRHS Collection)*

The two-story Italianate structure at **Berwyn** (MP 17.5) was built in 1881, one of a small number of all-brick stations on the Main Line. The frame cover shed (Type W-33) was extended in 1906, and the westbound shelter (Type W-36) was built in 1912. Although it isn't apparent here, the station is located at the westward end of a sharp four-degree curve, with a less sharp reverse curve east of that. Realignment of the right-of-way to the south in a broad sweeping curve was proposed as part of the 1902 Improvements program, but was of lower priority than Penn Station in New York City and new stations in North and West Philadelphia, so it was never carried out. This view provides a good look at the main structure as it appeared on August 10, 2001, with new canopy roof material. *(Dr. Art Peterson)*

The wood frame shelter (Type W-35 with curved brackets) at **Daylesford** (MP 18.6) was built on the edge of the fill above Lancaster Avenue. This view looking westward in June 1967 shows several young girls eagerly awaiting the next train. What roared by (opposite page) made them back away! *(Both- Frank Watson)*

And now we come to **Paoli** (MP 19.8), the final stop of countless numbers of "Paoli Locals." The main station was a two-story frame structure (Type 2W-6) built on the edge of a cut above the tracks on the eastbound side in 1883. A frame platform shelter (Type W-35) was added at track level in 1898. This view looks westward in April 1968 as an eastbound MU train pauses at the replacement station, a utilitarian one-story brick structure built in 1953. Paoli was named after a tavern honoring General Pasqulale di Paoli, an early Corsican patriot and leader.

(William Rosenberg)

A westbound shelter (Type W-35) was built in 1898 and extended in 1909. When the new station was constructed, the trackside shelter on the westbound side was replaced with a matching brick structure, but the covered stairway and the upper portion of the original shelter were retained. Westbound Amtrak Train #41 THE BROADWAY LIMITED pauses at the shelter in June 1973.

The bottom view nicely framed by the Valley Road overpass bridge provides a look at the layout of the facilities west of the station in February 1975. At the far right is a single-story brick section house and yardmaster's office. Beyond that is Paoli Tower and farther down the line is another concrete substation built in 1915. Behind the tower is the MU Storage Yard leading to the shops. *(Both- Will Coxey, West Jersey Chapter NRHS Collection)*

Train #31 THE NATIONAL LIMITED crosses over from Track #4 to 3 at **Paoli Tower** (MP 19.9) on May 6, 1972. The two-story brick and frame structure was built in 1896. As built it had a curved operator's bay with windows on the lower story facing the track. This view shows the west side along with repairs underway to the south wall damaged by a wreck crane being moved in a freight – reportedly too fast – in January of that year. *(William Rosenberg)*

The tower housed a 56-lever mechanical machine plus a 23-lever electro-pneumatic machine. It controlled the complete set of crossovers on the mainline, but its main task was to control the frequent movements of MU cars in and out of both ends of the yard. Here we get a closer look at the east and north sides of the tower, revealing a small concrete shed with a cast-on keystone over the door, used to house electrical equipment. The MU storage yard was clear enough in December 1971 to see the MP54's in the distance alongside the shops. *(William Rosenberg)*

The Paoli area always attracted visiting rail photographers as the combination of signal tower, storage yard, station and heavy rail traffic provided many intriguing combinations. Let's take a look the efforts of three veterans.

In June 1973, Will Coxey took advantage of the long day and Valley Road overpass to capture this captivating look at the sun setting on a westbound MU train bypassing the almost empty MU yard. By the end of the evening, every track would be full.
(Will Coxey, West Jersey Chapter NRHS Collection)

In March 1969, local resident Frank Watson was trackside to capture this most unusual power consist heading a freight west. Five GG1's could mean a road failure/rescue or power balancing. At this late date, the reader is invited to draw his own conclusions. *(Frank Watson)*

Always happy to incorporate a handsome signal tower into one of his compositions, New Jerseyan Bill Brennan took up a position just west of Paoli Tower late on a June 1969 afternoon to see what the railroad might provide.

First an RS3/DL701 "snapper" combination was returning east after making a shove from Philadelphia. The 5401 was a very late production RS3 (1956) still retaining its distinctive PRR billboard number indicators up front.

The long June day permitted Bill to catch the real prize of the day – THE BROADWAY LIMITED. It was nearly 8 p.m. as Train #49 accelerated from the station stop on Track #4.

(Both- William J. Brennan)

The **Paoli Car Shop** was built in 1915 to maintain the MP54 fleet operating on the newly-electrified Main Line into Broad Street Station. The one-story brick and concrete structure, which replaced a brick enginehouse and steam locomotive shop built in 1865, measured 282' long and 110' wide. Here strings of MP54's await service in the facility in December 1974. West of the shop a tail track and duckunder were built in 1906 that allows equipment to move under the mainline and head eastward without crossing over the four-track mainline.
(Will Coxey, West Jersey Chapter NRHS Collection)

Inside the venerably facility, more than 50 years after construction, MP54's still are serviced in October 1967. The shop had five run-through tracks with service pits – two tracks served by an overhead crane for lifting cars needing major repairs. The facility was also equipped with a blacksmith shop, machine shop, electric motor shop and an air brake shop, plus a storage area and foreman's office. Conrail took over operation of the shop from Penn Central on April 1, 1976. It was turned over to SEPTA on January 1, 1983 when that organization took control of all commuter operations in the Philadelphia area. *(William Rosenberg)*

We now move westward to Whitford (MP 28.2), formerly Oakland, the location of early iron mines and lime kilns as well as marble quarries used in the construction of numerous buildings in Philadelphia. Looking eastward in October 1990 at approaching Philadelphia to Harrisburg Train #603 provides an opportunity to review the station. The compact one-story frame structure (Type W-3) was built in 1907 in the shadow of the bridge. During a typical weekday it is surrounded by commuters' cars filling the small parking area. At one time a small coal trestle was located east of the station. Train #603 rides on Track #4, the westward main as the author/photographer stands on the roadbed of Track #3, removed due to the decline in both freight and passenger traffic. *(Robert J. Yanosey)*

And now the bridge. The massive (it's hard to avoid using that word for it) 373' long steel Pennsylvania Truss (**Bridge 28.85**) was erected in 1904 to carry the Low-Grade freight line (Philadelphia & Thorndale Branch) over the Main Line. The bridge is instantly identifiable to fans as the location for the Grif Teller painting *Main Lines – Freight and Passenger*, the 1949 PRR calendar subject.

(Morning Sun Books Collection)

At this point the main is descending westward through the East Brandywine Valley into Downingtown, and the jumpover allowed the Cutoff to maintain a level grade as it followed the shoulder of the South Valley Hills – a magnificent example of PRR engineering prowess! This view made from the bridge shows the freight Cutoff at left and the passenger main at right – Train #606 (Harrisburg-Philadelphia) consisting of lone Silverliner II #213 moves eastward on February 22, 1967. Note the electrification on the Cutoff, a feature which the Grif Teller painting somehow omitted. *(William M. Tilden)*

Moving farther westward we come to **Thorn Tower** (MP 35.0), the control facility for the central portion of the trackage east of Lancaster. The two-story brick structure was built in 1938, consolidating Glen, Dale, Downs and Caln interlockings at the point where the P&T Low-Grade freight line (Trenton Cutoff) joined the mainline. E44's #4432 and 4428 move coal tonnage eastward from Enola Yard past the tower in April 1970. *(Gerald Landau Collection)*

The two-story brick station pictured here in October 1995 is the third built to serve the industrial city of **Coatesville** (MP 38.4), the home of iron foundries and steel mills in the West Brandywine Valley beginning in the 1790s. The first station was built by the P&C west of town at a place known as Midway because it was equidistant between Philadelphia and Columbia. The second station was built in 1858, located farther east on Railroad Avenue between First and Second Avenues, and the third was constructed in 1869 a short distance still further east at Third Avenue. The first view shows the eastward end of the structure, revealing the extension added in 1907. The second view on the same date shows the westward end, which was also extended. At one time the central portion was a full three stories with peaked roof and Italianate details. *(Both- Dr. Art Peterson)*

Park Tower (MP 43.9) is a one-story brick structure built in 1938 on the eastbound side of the right-of-way. It housed a 39-lever electro-pneumatic machine that controlled a complex series of crossovers leading to a duck under west of the passenger station that allowed the freight tracks to separate from the passenger mainline and continue westward on the Low-Grade Line (Atglen & Susquehanna Branch). This view shows the building in use by Amtrak as a maintenance facility on July 27, 2000.

(Dr. Art Peterson)

Parkesburg (MP 44.2) was the location of early and thus little-known shops of the P&C that were replaced in 1861 by new facilities constructed by PRR in Harrisburg. The station was built on the eastbound side in 1906 at the time of the Low-Grade Line track realignment through the area, replacing an earlier frame depot built in 1896. As built, the one-story brick structure (a perfect example of a Type B-4) had a central brick tower, subsequently removed. This view looking eastward in June 1986 shows a fan trip utilizing ex-Reading MU equipment. At this location the passenger tracks are on the outside and the freight tracks are in the center. The Division Post with the Harrisburg Division is at MP 45.0, just to the west. *(Harold A. Smith)*

While the Main Line commuter district ended at Paoli, Philadelphia Division stations at Whitford, Downingtown, Coatesville and Parkesburg still retained a minimal level of commuter service. This October 1964 PRR Form 40 timetable has only one of its ten panels devoted to Parkesburg-Philadelphia service.
(Morning Sun Books Collection)

Why is a photo of a lowly **telegraph pole** included in a book on railroad facilities? Well, first of all the array of at least seven double crossarms on the weathered pole makes an interesting photographic subject. As in all things, PRR had precise standards for telegraph poles and all associated accoutrements: Chestnut was the wood of choice in 25', 30', or 35' lengths; crossarms were 10' with wood pins and aerial wire #110 or #9 copper. But more importantly to the reader of these volumes, telegraph communication was a vital – and in the early years, the only – means of communication between the railroad's facilities. PRR was closely associated with the development of telegraph communication, especially along the east-west main, which was later supplemented by the telephone and subsequently replaced by two-way radio. But the lineside telegraph infrastructure grew to the extent depicted here and remained in place long after its usefulness had been overtaken by newer technologies. So let this August 1984 view of a survivor be our tribute to railroad telegraph communication – and the lowly, but necessary, physical facilities it utilized. *(Emery Gulash, Morning Sun Books Collection)*

TRENTON BRANCH

HISTORICAL BACKGROUND

The double-track Trenton Cutoff (later Branch) was built by PRR in 1890-92 to bypass Philadelphia, primarily to relieve the congested West Philadelphia (52nd Street) Yards of heavy eastbound New York City coal traffic. The line ran from Morrisville Yard, just south of Trenton on the New York Division, to a junction with the Schuylkill Division at Earnest, completed in 1891. The remaining portion of the line connecting with the mainline at Glen Loch was opened in the following year. After completion of the Low-Grade Line extending west to Enola, the Trenton Cutoff was upgraded with reduced grades and improved bridges to conform to Low-Grade standards. The line was used almost exclusively for freight, although for a short period it carried passenger trains running via the Chestnut Hill Branch. It was electrified in 1938 and became the haunt of P5a's and later E44's.

Interlocking	Interlocking Station	Block Station	Block-Limit Station	TRENTON BRANCH	
X	X	X-O		MORRIS	4
X	X			MY ▼	4
X				MB ★/R-Morris	4
		X		COPPER ▼R-Morris	4
				NICKEL	4
X				MA★R-Morris	4
				DIVISION POST (N.Y.-Phila. Div.)	3
				LANGHORNE	3
				ROXTON	3
				HEATON	2
				DRESHER	2
				FORT HILL	2
				WHITEMARSH	2
				TB-16	
				PLYMOUTH MEETING	1
		X-O		NEST	1
				EARNEST	1
				RAMBO	
				TB-20	
				TB-22	
				KING	
				HOWELLVILLE	
X				DALE—R-Thorn	
X				GLEN—R-Thorn	

With no passenger trains in recent decades, few stations and perhaps a general unawareness of its operations, the Trenton Cutoff was seldom photographed. However, we have provided these two views. The first shows a pair of E44's leading a westbound freight across **Bridge 21.91** over the Reading's Bethlehem Branch, later the SEPTA line to Lansdale. This "temporary" wooden trestle replaced a through truss bridge that had been destroyed in a derailment and subsequent conflagration in July 1956. A permanent steel girder replacement bridge was finally installed by Conrail in 1976. The Pennsylvania Turnpike is in the background of this spring 1961 view. *(Al Holtz)*

This November 20, 1948 view shows the trim freight station at **Plymouth Meeting** (MP 17.6 from Dale interlocking). The one-story frame structure was built in 1897 at the eastern end of the Earnest Yard complex, located at the junction with the Schuylkill Division. The town derived its name from the Quaker meeting house located there.

(James P. Shuman)

SCHUYLKILL BRANCH

HISTORICAL BACKGROUND

The Pennsylvania Schuylkill Valley Railroad was constructed beginning in 1881 and extending up the valley deep into previously exclusive and sacrosanct Reading Company territory. Construction of the line was championed by PRR President George Roberts ostensibly to tap the local industries in the valley, but a second objective was to gain a more direct access to the anthracite coalfields that PRR had acquired in the 1870s. Both businesses were in direct competition with the Reading during a period of conflict between the two roads. A short branch from the main at Frazer north to Phoenixville was begun in 1881, and construction of the primary route began in the following year at the junction with the mainline at 52nd Street, reaching as far north as Pottsville by 1886. The line was then extended to Boston Junction (later Newton) by purchasing the Pottsville & Mahanoy Railroad and utilizing trackage rights on the LV to reach the coalfields in 1887.

Although the line was 50 years late and had to settle for the second-best route up the valley, it initially prospered, albeit always in the shadow of the Reading. It reached its peak in both freight and passenger traffic between the world wars, but gradually declining thereafter. PRR divested its coal properties by 1917, although the line continued to haul significant, but eventually declining, anthracite traffic for years afterwards. The lower end of the line was electrified as far as Norristown in 1930 as part of the Philadelphia Improvements, the final extension of suburban electrification. However, passenger service west of Norristown was Sunday-only after 1941 and discontinued entirely 10 years later.

Wynnefield Avenue (MP 4.9 from Suburban Station) was a two-story structure built within the city limits that, like several others on the branch, housed passenger, baggage and freight facilities when it opened in 1896. The station had seen better days when this eastward view was recorded in March 1962. *(John Dziobko, Jr.)*

Interlocking	Interlocking Station	Block Station	Block-Limit Station	SCHUYLKILL BRANCH		Distance from Sub. Sta., Phila.
X				VALLEY—R-Overbrook		4.0
X				JEFF—R-Overbrook		4.5
				WYNNEFIELD AVE.	Schuylkill Branch	4.9
				BALA		5.7
				CYNWYD		6.1
				BARMOUTH		6.8
				MANAYUNK		7.8
X			X	MAN—R-Overbrook		8.2
				SHAWMONT		9.6
				MIQUON		10.8
				SPRING MILL		12.4
				CONSHOHOCKEN		13.6
				IVY ROCK		15.1
				EARNEST		15.9
X	X	X-O		NORRIS		16.5
				NORRISTOWN		17.5
			X	HAWS AVE.—R-Norris		18.1
				PORT INDIAN		20.1
				BETZWOOD		21.8
X-A				CREEK (Reading Co. Crossing)		24.6
				OAKS		24.8
				PHOENIXVILLE		28.1
				CROMBY		30.4
				SPRING CITY		32.3
				PARKERFORD		35.1
			X	LOCK—C-Norris		37.8
				POTTSTOWN		40.3
				MONOCACY		46.7
				DYER		47.2
				BIRDSBORO		49.1
X	X	X-O		BROOKE (Reading Co. Xing)	Schuylkill Secondary Track	58.3
				READING		62.8
				GROUNDS		64.2
				TEMPLE		67.1
			X	ORCHARD—C-Norris		67.7
				LEESPORT		71.7
				SHOEMAKERSVILLE		76.8
			X	HAMBURG—C-Norris		84.8
				AUBURN		88.0
				ADAMSDALE		88.7
			X	ADAM—C-Norris		90.6
				SCHUYLKILL HAVEN		93.5
				CARBON		94.7
				POTTSVILLE		95.6
			X	ULMER—C-Norris		97.5
				ST. CLAIR		99.7
				MORRIS		102.1
				ROCK		104.6
				NEW BOSTON		
			X	NEWTON—C-Norris	L.V.R.R.	162.9
X	B	B		LAUREL JCT.		157.7

The stately two-story frame station and agent's quarters at **Bala** (MP 5.7) retains at least some of it dignity in this March 1965 view. It was built in 1884 to serve a growing PRR-developed suburban community named by Miriam Roberts, President George Roberts' second wife after his ancestor's origin in Bala, Wales. The station was enlarged at the near (westward) end in 1909, nearly doubling its size and grouping it under Type 2W-6. The overpass bridge in the background carries City Line Avenue. *(John Dziobko, Jr.)*

The brick and frame structure (Type 2B-1) serving **Cynwyd** (MP 6.1) (pronounced kinwid) was built in 1890 as a combination station for passenger, baggage and freight traffic. The community was originally known as Academyville, but changed its name to comply with PRR's designated Welsh appellation for the station stop. This eastward view made in March 1965 shows the station as enlarged in 1909, with a nice example of a Type W-36 shelter shed. *(John Dziobko, Jr.)*

Barmouth (MP 6.8) was not an early stop on the Schuylkill Valley Branch. The initial station serving the area was built a short distance away at West Laurel Hill, near the cemetery of the same name. That station was closed and the agency moved to Barmouth in 1899, where a one-story brick structure (similar to Type B-4, with a center tower and a two-story agent's residence on the westward end) was constructed. This structure was torn down and replaced with this shelter and extended canopy recorded in March 1962. *(Both- John Dziobko, Jr.)*

In July 1963, Silverliner II #204 pauses for business. Barmouth is another Welsh name, but one with railroad heritage. Barmouth Bridge is a famous single-track wooden bridge in North Wales crossing Cardigan Bay.

(David Cope)

Bridge 7.70, better known as the Schuylkill River Bridge, is shown here in a view looking west along the Schuylkill Expressway on June 12, 1965. The massive 1818' long concrete arch viaduct was built in 1917 at a cost of nearly $1 million and was the largest on the branch. It replaced the original 14-span deck truss and girder structure with wooden trestle approaches built in 1883 in a bridge improvement program that allowed PRR to use heavier locomotives on the branch.

(James P. Shuman)

The Reading's Manayunk freight house at the eastern end of the concrete apron and under the one-half plate girder approach spans marks the path of the electrified double-track Reading's Norristown Branch, shown here in August 1973. Construction of the new PRR bridge required realignment of both the PRR and Reading through this area.

(William Rosenberg)

The eastbound **Manayunk** (MP 7.8) passenger shelter was built in 1917 at the western end of the new bridge. A November 1966 view shows the intertwined relationship between the PRR Schuylkill Branch and Reading's Norristown Branch at this point. *(Emery Gulash, Morning Sun Books Collection)*

Manayunk was an early industrial community in the valley settled along the Schuylkill Canal in 1819, the location of early flour, paper and textile mills powered by a dam upriver. The canal, which passed along the edge of town, also brought abundant raw materials including iron ore, limestone and hardwood to an early iron foundry located just west of town.

This March 1962 view looks back at the westward end of the eastbound shelter. This structure (a variant of Type W-37) was connected by a stairway and subway under the tracks to the westbound waiting room and shelter on the opposite side. When the new bridge was constructed, both of these structures replaced the original two-story station (Type 2B-2) built in 1890. *(John Dziobko, Jr.)*

Nestled against the base of the last arch on the westward (Manayunk) end of the Schuylkill River Bridge is this old **PRR Substation**, subsequently utilized as an antique shop by the time this photo was made on April 26, 1975. The structure, most likely built when the line was electrified in 1930, featured extensive brick detailing highlighted in this view.
(Harold A. Smith)

After some 30 years of MP54 service on the lower section of the Schuylkill Branch, the introduction of new Silverliner cars was an event not to be ignored. Consequently, they adorned schedules of most Philadelphia Division commuter lines. "Operation Manayunk" was a special $.30 promotional fare between Manayunk and PRR Philadelphia stations or a $.40 fare in combination with PTC created with the aid of the City of Philadelphia to increase ridership.
(Morning Sun Books Collection)

This small brick shelter serving **Shawmont** (MP 9.5), shown in an August 1964 view, replaced the original small frame station and shelter shed built in 1884. The passenger and freight agency was closed in 1913 and transferred to Manayunk, but trains continued to stop for the convenience of passengers.
(John Dziobko, Jr.)

Miquon (MP 10.8) was another small station stop utilizing a Type W-35 frame shelter, shown here as it appeared in August 1964. *(John Dziobko, Jr.)*

These two views dated March 1965 show the attractive two-story brick and frame station and agent's residence (Type 2B-1) built in 1884 at **Spring Mill** (MP 12.4). The first view shows the saw tooth wood shingles on the upper portion of the main structure repeated on the end of the cover shed (Type W-33).

The second view shows (in addition to the two '57 Chevys) the extremely close proximity of the Reading's Norristown Branch, which utilized an adjacent right-of-way through this area. This situation led to several instances of corporate conflict during construction of the PRR line. PRR usually prevailed although by the time the two lines were electrified, they cooperated on erection of the side-by-side catenary systems. *(Both- John Dziobko, Jr.)*

This brick structure was originally the freight house serving **Conshohocken** (MP 13.6), another location of early industries along the Schuylkill Canal and later the site of the massive Alan Wood Steel complex located just west of town on both sides of the river. A two-story brick passenger station (Type B-3, with high dormer windows) was built here in 1884. By the time of this March 1965 view, the passenger station had been demolished and the freight structure used for the remaining passengers.

Earnest (MP 15.9) was the point where the Trenton Cutoff crossed over the Schuylkill Branch. The two lines connected via a wye leading to Earnest Yard located alongside the freight line, which was on a high fill with deck truss bridges spanning the river and both rail lines below. This view shows a westbound fan trip passing the small frame shelter shed (Type W-35), boarded up, but still proudly displaying its keystone station sign on June 12, 1955. The Trenton Cutoff is visible in the background through the maze of high-voltage lines.

Norris Tower (MP 16.5) was a two-story frame structure that contained a 24-lever mechanical machine and a 10-lever table unit that controlled movements through the Norristown station to the west, a small freight yard at this location and the wye junction with the Trenton Cutoff to the east discussed above. This slightly soft view looks westward at the tower and small yard office on the same date. *(All- John Dziobko, Jr.)*

Norristown (MP 17.5), the county seat of Montgomery County, has been served by a total of four PRR passenger stations during its history. The first was a two-story brick structure (Type 2B-2) built in 1884 on Lafayette Street at the corner of DeKalb Street. This building was followed by the second, a two-story brick and stone facility built in 1904 half a block to the west along Lafayette Street to reduce blocking the busy DeKalb Street crossing. After several fatal accidents at this crossing and some 15 years of deliberation, both PRR and the Reading responded to public pressure and agreed that the grade crossings through the area had to be eliminated, but refused to share a joint passenger station. So they built two new passenger and freight stations.

The Norristown Improvements, as they were called, eventually resulted in the relocation and elevation of both roads, eliminating seven grade crossings through the downtown area.

The one-story brick station shown here in this May 1961 view was built in 1934 facing Lafayette Street between DeKalb and Swede Streets. A high-level concrete platform extended 550' between two main tracks, with a 40' long brick shelter serving both tracks. A pedestrian tunnel under both rights-of-way connected the PRR and Reading stations. The structure spanning both tracks in this view is the Philadelphia & Western interurban transit line, later known as SEPTA's Norristown High-Speed Line, whose station is just to the right. *(John Dziobko, Jr.)*

As is usually the case where a line is only partially-electrified, passenger traffic and service west of Norristown was minimal. In a rare August 1947 Kodachrome, a rail motorcar and trailer get underway for Reading. The 1934 station improvements included a "pocket" track for easy transfer between the electrified MP54 trains and steam or rail motorcar trains operating west of Norristown. *(Robert Fillman)*

The fourth Norristown station was built a short distance to the west in 1903 at Franklin Avenue, later designated **Haws Avenue** (MP 18.1). An engine house, coaling facility and turntable were also constructed at this location, which subsequently became the end of the electrified zone on the branch and later a diesel service area. This view shows the one-story brick structure in August 1964.

(John Dziobko, Jr.)

PRR constructed this attractive two-story brick station (similar to Type 2B-2) to serve the prosperous industrial community of **Phoenixville** (MP 28.1), location of the massive Phoenix Iron Works (later Phoenix Iron and Steel). This station, with its open shelter (similar to Type W-36) at track level, became known for its award-winning landscaped grounds including extensive flowerbeds. This 1908 postcard view looks eastward on the line along the shoulder of Black Rock Hill. At right is Phoenix Tower, which controlled PRR movements in and out of the Iron Works in the valley below as well as the junction with the Frazer Branch just west of the station. After passenger service was discontinued in the mid-1950s, the station was used for freight, replacing the former frame freight station on the other side of town served by the Frazer Branch.

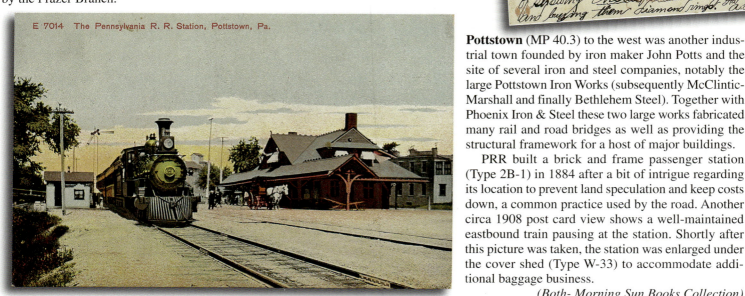

Pottstown (MP 40.3) to the west was another industrial town founded by iron maker John Potts and the site of several iron and steel companies, notably the large Pottstown Iron Works (subsequently McClintic-Marshall and finally Bethlehem Steel). Together with Phoenix Iron & Steel these two large works fabricated many rail and road bridges as well as providing the structural framework for a host of major buildings.

PRR built a brick and frame passenger station (Type 2B-1) in 1884 after a bit of intrigue regarding its location to prevent land speculation and keep costs down, a common practice used by the road. Another circa 1908 post card view shows a well-maintained eastbound train pausing at the station. Shortly after this picture was taken, the station was enlarged under the cover shed (Type W-33) to accommodate additional baggage business.

(Both- Morning Sun Books Collection)

Birdsboro (MP 49.1) was another town with early iron furnaces and later steel mills. This interesting and useful view from Brooke Tower shows the layout of the PRR and Reading stations as they appeared on January 23, 1974. At left is the PRR passenger station, a two-story brick and frame structure (Type 2B-1) built in 1887 shown here converted to apartments with a bar and pizzeria on the first floor. In the background at right is the PRR freight house, with the Reading station in front that served the Reading's Wilmington & Northern Branch. *(Rich Taylor)*

Brooke Tower (MP 49.2) was a two-story frame Reading Company facility (BE) shared by PRR to control the crossing of the Schuylkill Valley by the Reading's W&N Branch that ran south to serve the large steel mill in Coatesville and then continued to Wilmington. To the west of the junction was a small Reading freight yard, with a wye leading to a track connecting the Reading Belt Line to the Reading mainline across the river. This westward view of the tower was made in April 1962. *(John Dziobko, Jr.)*

Here we have a closer look at the **Birdsboro Freight House** as it appeared in November 1974. It was built in 1887 (a variant of Type W-18) and extended in 1913. Topped off with a ready roof, it measured 20' x 70' x 17.8'. Time and weather have taken their toll, but the beauty of the paneled siding and roof brackets remains. *(Both- George Berisso)*

Reading (MP 58.3) was still another sizeable iron and steel center served by both PRR and its namesake railroad. After protracted and acrimonious negotiations with the city and the Reading Company centered on the old wooden Penn Street Bridge, PRR finally agreed to rebuild the bridge. PRR utilized a temporary station when the line was opened in 1884, but settled the matter by purchasing the Reading's former Wilmington & Northern station located just west of the new bridge. The large 54 x 146' brick facility included an imposing Queen Anne style office building at the southward end that was used to house the Schuylkill Division superintendent and general offices.

When the city announced plans to construct a new concrete arch structure for Penn Street in 1912 (**Bridge 58.30**), the bridge again became a point of contention. Finally PRR agreed to demolish the office portion and relocate the offices to a new building nearby. The remaining portion of the station is just visible under the arch at left as G5s #1813 prepares to depart with Train #686 the Sunday-only local to Philadelphia in this early 1950s view. **Reading Tower** ("RA") facilitated train movements in this congested area. On Sunday, October 4, 1953 E6 #1600 and two P70's operating as Trains #685 and 585 ended Norristown-Reading passenger service. *(Frank Watson)*

The PRR **Reading Freight House** was a one-story frame structure (an extended version of Type W-18) located on Front Street south of the Penn Street overpass. It was later used as a carpenter shop and is shown here as it appeared during Penn Central days in November 1970.

(Richard Taylor)

The station serving **Shoemakersville** (MP 71.7) was typical of several north of Reading, a two-story frame structure similar to Type 2W-6 with agent's quarters on the second story. It was built in 1892 and is shown here converted to a private residence in this June 2000 view. At least it survives! The town was named after the Shoemaker family, who were outspoken in promoting the mining and use of anthracite as a clean-burning fuel.
(Dr. Art Peterson)

Mt. Carbon Enginehouse was nestled ("squeezed" might be a better term) in the narrow area between Sharp and Second Mountains. PRR constructed a yard in the old canal bed in 1884 and located an enginehouse, turntable and water tank on the graded area. The 11-stall roundhouse was finished in 1907. The yard was located just south of Pottsville (MP 94.7), the last community served by the line. In later years the end of track was 2400' west of MP 95.0. Unfortunately we don't have a color image of the passenger station, an imposing two-story brick structure with a center spire built in 1886. This Consolidation was sitting outside the enginehouse in the summer of 1951. *(Bruce Kantner)*

Carbon (MP 93.5 – formerly Mt. Carbon) was another area of close proximity and thus conflict with the Reading, which tried to block construction of the PRR line, both physically and in the courts. PRR prevailed on all counts.

A popular fan trip powered by a trio of EP20's wound its way of the line on June 12, 1955, two years after passenger service had been discontinued west of Norristown. Photographer John Dziobko captured these two views of the two-story frame station, standpipe and two vintage wooden water tanks. *(Both- John Dziobko, Jr.)*

At Pottsville, the PRR fanned out to serve the anthracite region via several branches. On the short seven-mile Minersville Branch, built in 1892 to serve three coal mines, we find our final notable PRR facility. After leaving Pottsville, the line ran through the St. Clair Tunnel and then ascended a 3.1 per cent grade which was the ruling grade on the branch often requiring helpers.

It then crossed the Mill Creek Valley on the **Darkwater Trestle**, a 530' long deck plate girder structure (Bridge 3.50) built in 1886-7. The top view shows a freight headed by a BS24m traversing the trestle in May 1961 while the bottom shows the 1955 excursion southbound. Wouldn't you have enjoyed being aboard?

(Arch and Bruce Kantner)

EASTERN REGION—Continued
PHILADELPHIA TERMINAL DIVISION—Continued

Dist. from Jer. City (Pass. Sta.)

Fairhill Branch — CONNECTING RAILWAY—Continued

FA
- Fairhill, Phila., Pa. (Freight Station and Public Delivery)‡ 82.1
- " (Standard Packing Box Co.)† 82.1
- " (Philco Corp. No. 4)† 82.1
- " (Cross Bros.)† 82.1
- " (Magee Bros.)† 82.3
- " (Philco Corp. No. 1)† 82.4
- " (Philco Corp. No. 2)† 82.4
- " (Smith Bros. No. 1 & 2)† 82.6
- " (Philco Corp. No. 3)† 82.6
- " (Western Elec. Co. Inc.)† 82.7
- North Penn, Phila., Pa. (Northeastern Warehouse Co.)† 82.3
- " (Public Delivery) 82.3
- " (Active Steel Co.)† 82.3
- " (R. B. Fritch & Co.)† 82.3
- " (Fletcher Works, Inc. No. 2)† 82.3
- " (Fletcher Works, Inc. No. 1)† 82.3
- " (Fletcher Works, Inc. No. 3)† 82.3
- " (SKF Industries Inc. No. 2—Atlas Ball Div.)† 82.3
- " (Pecora Paint Co. Inc.)† 82.3
- " (S. L. Allen & Co.)† 82.4
- " (Russell & Smith Co. and Cambria Iron & Metal Co.)† 82.6
- " (Sixth St. Yard)‖ 82.6
- " (Stern Co. No. 1)† 82.6
- " (Stern & Co. No. 2 — Johnson Whse.)† 82.8

83
- " (Ninth St. Yard)‖ 82.9
- " (Surpass Leather Co. and Penn Mutual Grocery Co. Inc.)† 83.0
- " (Atlantic Refining Co. No. 1)† 83.0
- " (Wm. J. Alexander & Sons)† 83.0
- " (Shippers Whse. Co.)† 83.0
- " (North American Lace Co.)† 83.0
- " (Twelfth St. Freight Yard) 83.1
- " (National Biscuit Co. No. 1)† 83.1
- " (National Biscuit Co. No. 2 & 3)† 83.1
- " (Wilen Bros. and Dickstein Flooring Co.)† 83.4
- " (Jos. J. Greenburg)† 83.4
- " (Autocar Company No. 2)† 83.4
- " (S. Margolis No. 3)† 83.1
- " (Bisceglia Bros. Corp.)† 83.1
- " (Broad St. Freight Yard) 83.2
- " (North Phila. Freight Station)‡ 83.3
- " (J. M. Bruner & Co. No. 1)† 83.3
- North Phila., Pa. (Station)‡‡ 83.5
- " (Jc. Reading Co.) 83.7
- " (Ward Baking Co. and Electric Service Supplies Co.)† 83.7

84
- " (International Harvester Co. Inc. No. 2 and Reyburn Mfg. Co.)† 83.7

† For individual use
‡ Telephone Office
‖ Siding—No carload delivery
‡ Telegraph Office

EASTERN REGION—Continued
PHILADELPHIA TERMINAL DIVISION—Continued

Dist. from Jer. City (Pass. Sta.)

Stifftown Branch — CONNECTING RAILWAY—Continued

- North Phila., Pa. (Eighteenth & Cambria Sts. Public Delivery) 83.7
- " (Linde Air Products Co.)† 83.7
- " (Storage) 83.7
- " (Chas. H. White & Sons.)† 83.7
- " (Erie Steel Co. Inc.)† 83.7
- " (M. L. Bayard & Co. Inc.)† 83.7
- " (James E. Tague Co.)† 83.7
- " (Ralph G. Spiegle & Co.)† 83.7
- " ("North Phila." Tower) 83.7
- " (Fifteenth St. Freight Yard) 83.8
- " (Merchants' Warehouse Co. No. 7)† 83.8
- " (Dunlop Tire & Rubber Co., E. H. Heydt, and Paramount Paper Products Co.)† 83.7
- " (Weil-McLain Co., Tri-State Distributors, Great American Tea Co. and Eastern Battery Separator Co.)† 83.8
- " (C. H. Wheeler Mfg. Co.)† 83.9
- " (Joseph Cohen & Sons)† 83.9
- " (North American Warehousing Co. No. 1)† 84.0
- " (Margie St. Classification Yard, North Side—E. Conn.) 84.0

84
- " (North American Warehousing Co. No. 2)† 84.0
- " (Este Delivery and Storage Yard) 84.0
- " (Food Fair, Inc.)† 84.1
- " (Scales) 84.1
- " (Derr-Gibbons Supply Co.)† 84.2
- " (Este Storage and Delivery Yard—West End) 84.4
- " (Margie St. Classification Yard—W. Conn.) 84.4
- " (S. S. Fretz Jr. Inc.)† 84.4
- " (Armstrong Cork Co. and Geo. Nass & Son Inc.)† 84.4
- " (Diamond St. Yard and Public Delivery) 84.8
- " (Borghesi Coal Co.)† 84.8
- " (William Nusbickel, Inc.)† 84.8
- " (Fleming & Bates Coal Co. No. 1)† 84.8
- " (John Williams No. 1)† 84.8
- " (John Williams No. 2)† 84.8
- " (A. M. Bealer Coal Co.)† 84.8
- " (Elam E. Whitman)† 84.8
- " (Standard Ice & Coal Co.)† 84.8
- " (Philip Carey Mfg. Co.)† 84.8
- " (Schuylkill Chemical Co.)† 84.8
- " (Wirt & Knox Mfg. Co.)† 84.8
- " (Thos. E. Coale Lumber Co.)† 84.8
- " (William H. Clausen)† 84.8
- " (Great Atlantic & Pacific Tea Co.)† 85.1
- " (Mason-Heflin Coal Co. No. 1 and Keystone Coal & Wood Co. No. 4)† 85.3
- " (Jc. Chestnut Hill Branch)*‡ 83.7

* No Siding
† For individual use
‡ Telegraph Office

EASTERN REGION—Continued
PHILADELPHIA TERMINAL DIVISION—Continued

Dist. from Jer. City (Pass. Sta.)

Chestnut Hill Branch—Midvale Br. — CONNECTING RAILWAY—Continued

- North Phila., Pa. (Victor Coal & Fuel Co. No. 3)† 84

1154
- " (Pittsburgh Plate Glass Co.)† 84
- " (Phila. Motor Accessories Co.)† 84
- " (Electric Storage Battery Co.)† 84
- Westmoreland, Phila., Pa. (Station) 84
- " (Westmoreland Public Delivery and American Ice Co. No. 2)† 84
- " (General Motors Corp. Nos. 1 & 2—Chevrolet Div.)† 84

1155
- " (Vermont Marble Co. and Pioneer Paper Stock Co.)† 84
- " (Edward G. Budd Mfg. Co. No. 1—"Dryer")† 84
- " (Edward G. Budd Mfg. Co. No. 2—"X" Bldg.)† 84
- " (Edward G. Budd Mfg. Co. No. 3—"Budd Wheel")† 84
- Midvale, Phila., Pa. (Edw. G. Budd Mfg. Co. (No. 4—"Simmons")† 84
- " (Edw. G. Budd Mfg. Co. No. 5—"House Track & West Side Spur")† 84
- " (Storage) 84

1155
- " (Edw. G. Budd Mfg. Co. No. 6—"Oil Spur & East Side Bldg.")† 85
- " (Edw. G. Budd Mfg. Co. No. 7—"Bomb Bldg.")† 85
- " (Edw. G. Budd Mfg. Co. No. 8—"Vim Bldg.")† 85

1156 Junction Midvale Branch‖ 85
- Midvale, Phila., Pa. (American Pulley Co. Nos. 1 & 2)† 85

1167
- " (Sinclair Refining Co. No. 2)† 85
- " (Midvale Co.—Interchange) 85
- " (Midvale Co.—Storage)‖ 85
- Midvale, Phila., Pa. (Morris, Wheeler & Co. No. 2 and Edw. G. Budd Mfg. Co. No. 9—"New Vim & T")† 85
- " (Monad Paint & Varnish Co.)† 85
- " (Midvale Yard—Lower)‖ 85

1157
- " (Bendix Aviation Corp.)† 85
- " (Freight Sta. and Public Delivery)‡ 85
- " (McCandlish Lithograph Corp.)† 85
- " (Midvale Yard—Upper)‖ 86
- " (U. S. Army—Phila. Signal Depot)† 86
- Queen Lane, Pa.*‡ 86
- Germantown, Pa. (Chelten Ave.)‡ 86
- " (Wister, Heberton Co.)† 86

1158
- " (Freight Station and Public Delivery and J. G. Robinson Inc.†) 86
- Tulpehocken, Pa.*‡ 87
- Upsal, Pa.*‡ 87

1159
- " (Keystone Coal & Wood Co. No. 5)† 87
- " (Germantown Steam Co.)† 87

1160 Carpenter, Pa. (Station and Public Delivery)‡ 88

* No Siding
† For individual use
‡ Telephone Office
‖ Siding—No carload delivery